spiritual spa

D1402444

spiritual spa

create a private sanctuary to refresh body and spirit

Gill Farrer-Halls

A GODSFIELD BOOK
www.godsfieldpress.com

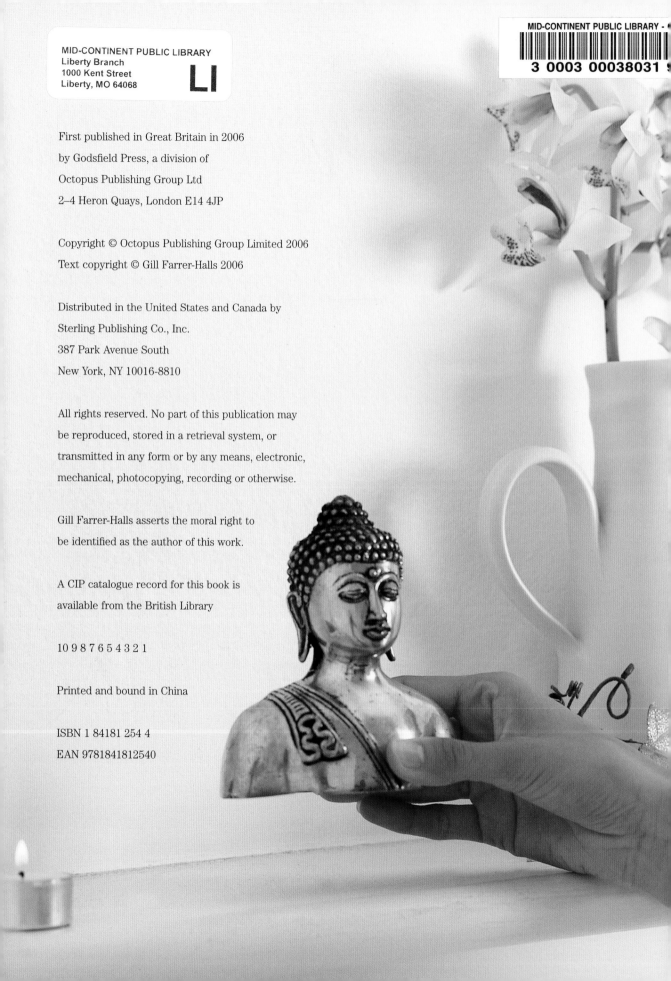

First published in Great Britain in 2006
by Godsfield Press, a division of
Octopus Publishing Group Ltd
2–4 Heron Quays, London E14 4JP

Distributed in the United States and Canada by
Sterling Publishing Co., Inc.
387 Park Avenue South
New York, NY 10016-8810

A CIP catalogue record for this book is
available from the British Library

10 9 8 7 6 5 4 3 2 1

Printed and bound in China

ISBN 1 84181 254 4
EAN 9781841812540

contents

introduction

Escaping from the stresses of everyday life is something we all dream of from time to time. However, other than an annual holiday, most of us never manage to find the time and space in our lives for serious rejuvenation. A retreat, or spiritual spa, offers you the opportunity to take time out from your daily routine, so that you literally 'retreat' or escape from the mundane activities of life.

why do a retreat at home?

Some people choose to stay at a residential health centre, or to visit a day spa, when they feel like escaping from the daily grind. This offers a good way to relax and feel reinvigorated. However, it is an expensive option that focuses on short-term, hedonistic luxuriating, and all too soon you have to face work and family commitments once again.

Others choose to undertake a retreat at one of the growing number of specialist centres that focus exclusively on meditation. This can facilitate a wonderfully calming, uplifting and spiritual experience, although the sometimes rather austere conditions at such centres do not encourage you to pay much attention to your body.

A combination of health spa and meditation centre offers a balance between calming the mind, refreshing the spirit and rejuvenating the body. An innovative idea is to create your own tailor-made spiritual spa at home as an alternative, or supplement, to holidays, health spas and meditation

Several meditation sessions are undertaken during each day of your home retreat to calm the mind.

centres. With a little preparation and determination, you can create a suitable environment at home in which to unwind and rejuvenate. This idea will appeal to everyone who is seeking some private time, rest and sanctuary from daily life, and who wishes to connect with his or her inner being.

benefits of a home retreat

The idea of undertaking a home retreat by yourself might at first sound a little daunting. What exactly is a 'retreat'? Retreats vary considerably, and are often highly specialized – for instance, there are dedicated retreats for yoga, t'ai chi, chi kung, meditation and prayer. More generally, a retreat may be defined as a quiet, private sanctuary from daily life. In this book you will find advice on how to create a personal 'spiritual spa' in the privacy of your own home – one that you have customized to meet your own needs.

The suggestions given here offer you ways to regenerate both mind and body and to reconnect with your spiritual essence. This holistic approach to revitalization provides an effective way to achieve good health, energy and inner peace. Focusing on all aspects of the self – mind, body and spirit – the various techniques and exercises seek to reunite these disparate parts into a balanced whole, making you ready once more to face the endless demands of everyday life.

Using ideas drawn from feng shui and aromatherapy, together with simple rituals, you will learn how to define the boundaries of your own personal sanctuary. Advice on how to minimize intrusions from other people, environmental noise and distractions will help you make your sanctuary a truly private and silent space. Emphasizing the

Yoga and other stretching and grounding exercises form an integral part of your spiritual spa experience.

simplicity and tranquillity found in traditional spiritual retreats, this book offers a variety of guided sitting and movement meditations, alongside instruction on easy stretching, chi kung and yoga exercises – all of which promote deep calm, harmony and spiritual well-being.

The importance of a simple but nourishing diet is reflected in the use of fresh, organic and vegetarian foods, as well as herbal teas. This healthy, detoxifying diet is combined with deep-cleansing techniques, and with baths and showers using essential oils. All these activities are incorporated into an easy-to-follow daily (or longer) programme. The book also offers tips on how to keep your resolve and make a firm commitment to complete your retreat, thereby deriving maximum benefit from it.

how to plan your retreat

Making a detailed plan – and sticking to it – forms the basis of a successful retreat. Without a proper plan and the personal commitment to keep to it, it is all too easy to fall by the wayside.

Many of us have made wonderful New Year resolutions to live healthy lives, perhaps by losing weight and cutting down on tea, coffee and alcohol, but after just a few days we slip back into our comfortable bad habits. Drawing up a formal plan or contract helps you stick to your original concept and see your spiritual spa through to the end.

Why is it so easy to abandon our plans and resolutions to be healthy, when this is what we really want to do? It's a bit simplistic to say that the means (dieting, meditating, exercising, detoxifying, and so on) are harder and less enjoyable than the end result: a calm, healthy, rejuvenated person. The most common reason for failed plans and New Year resolutions is the lack of proper preparation and planning. So spending time before your home retreat preparing yourself thoroughly, offers you a good chance of completing it successfully.

The process of making a commitment to a schedule helps you decide whether you have a real and serious intention to follow through your plans properly, or whether you just have a vague sense that a retreat sounds like a good idea. There is not much point in creating a spiritual sanctuary at home with a half-hearted attitude. Unless you have the solemn intention to follow through your home

Careful planning and preparation will enhance your retreat experience and reaffirm your aims.

retreat to the end, you need either to generate a sincere wish to complete it or to realize that perhaps now is not the right time for you to undertake such a venture.

Once you've made a formal commitment to a home retreat, you need to make some decisions.

These include: how many days your retreat will last; what all the different daily activities will consist of; when is a good time to begin your undertaking; and so on. At the end of this introduction, suggestions are given on how you can integrate some of the retreat activities into your daily life.

It is a good idea to start by doing a simple one-day home retreat that incorporates a range of basic activities. This will help you develop confidence, and will ensure that creating a spiritual spa at home is what you really want to do. Then you can move on to doing a longer retreat incorporating a wider range of activities with confidence and experience.

longer retreats

A longer retreat might last for two or three days, or up to a week. Unless you have already done several in-depth, teacher-led retreats, it is best not to undertake a home retreat lasting more than a week. A longer retreat would, typically, start with the basic one-day schedule (see page 10) for the first day, then progress to one, two or more classic one-day schedules (see page 11), and finish by repeating the basic one-day schedule. Activities and food can be varied, and various options for exercises, meditations and meals are described later on in the book.

incorporating retreat activities into daily life

You can easily select a particular meditation, and a yoga, t'ai chi or chi kung exercise, and try to do these each day as part of your daily routine. In this way you develop good habits that are beneficial to your well-being. For example, you could meditate

Placing beautiful, spiritually inspiring objects on a bathroom shelf creates a wonderful atmosphere.

every morning before going to work, so that you face the day ahead with a calm, focused mind. In the evening you could do some simple yoga exercises to stretch and ease tired muscles and let go of the day's tensions. Relaxing baths with essential oils, and healthy meals, can also be incorporated easily into your daily life.

daily schedules

The basic schedule, given below, is designed for those who want a simple retreat day. The classic schedule, see opposite, is suitable for those who have done some meditation and who want a more in-depth experience.

basic one-day schedule ✦

early morning

08.00 get up and shower, after using a natural exfoliating body scrub with essential oils

08.30 drink a glass of hot water with freshly squeezed lemon juice to stimulate and detoxify the liver

08.45 simple stretching exercises

09.00 calm meditation

09.30 breakfast of fruit, yogurt and muesli, with a cup of herbal tea

late morning

10.00 rest

10.30 re-energizing exercises

11.00 mindfulness meditation

11.30 cup of stimulating herbal tea

11.45 healing meditation using visualization

12.15 rest

afternoon

12.30 prepare vegetables and tofu (or soak beans) and brown rice for lunch

13.00 cook and eat lunch

14.00 rest

14.30 brisk, vigorous walk

15.15 calm meditation

15.45 cup of herbal tea

16.00 write about your feelings and experiences, in creative free writing or journaling exercise

16.30 insight meditation

17.00 rest

evening

17.30 prepare vegetables and make soup, dry-roast a handful of nuts and seeds, then mix with a handful of dried fruit

18.00 mindfulness meditation

18.30 eat supper with a cup of herbal tea

19.00 rest

19.15 walking meditation

19.45 loving-kindness meditation

20.15 relaxing exercises

20.45 bath with essential oils

21.15 meditation on watching the light fade (may be moved to earlier in the evening, depending on your location and the time of year)

21.45 chanting, mantra meditation or prayers

22.15 bedtime, with a cup of calming herbal tea

classic one-day schedule ✱

early morning

06.30 get up and shower, after using a natural exfoliating body scrub with essential oils

07.00 drink a glass of hot water with freshly squeezed lemon juice to stimulate and detoxify the liver

07.15 Salutation to the dawn yoga exercise

07.30 calm meditation

08.00 breakfast of fruit, yogurt and muesli, with a cup of herbal tea

late morning

08.30 rest

09.00 skin brushing to stimulate the circulation

09.30 mindfulness meditation

10.00 free dance

10.30 cup of stimulating herbal tea

10.45 healing meditation using visualization

11.15 rest

afternoon

11.30 prepare vegetables and tofu (or soak beans) and brown rice for lunch

12.00 cook and eat lunch

13.00 rest

13.30 brisk, vigorous walk

14.15 calm meditation

14.45 walking meditation

15.15 cup of herbal tea

15.30 re-energizing exercises

16.00 write about your feelings and experiences, in creative free writing or journaling exercise

16.30 insight meditation

17.00 relaxing exercises

evening

17.30 prepare vegetables and make soup, dry-roast a handful of nuts and seeds, then mix with a handful of dried fruit

18.00 calm meditation

18.30 eat supper with a cup of herbal tea

19.00 simple yoga stretching exercises

19.30 mindfulness meditation

20.00 relaxing exercises

20.30 loving-kindness meditation

21.00 bath with essential oils

21.30 meditation on watching the light fade (may be moved to earlier in the evening, depending on your location and the time of year)

22.00 chanting, mantra meditation or prayers

22.30 bedtime, with a cup of calming herbal tea

basic activities are indicated by ◆

classic activities are indicated by ✱

preparing for a retreat

When you are planning your home retreat it is vital to allot enough time to making thorough preparations. If you have ever attended a retreat centre or health spa, you may have noticed that there are quite a lot of people around the place who are dedicated to making your stay easy and pleasant. They ensure that the space is clean and welcoming, and supply food and all other necessary items to allow you to focus fully on your meditation, yoga or health and beauty treatments.

When creating a spiritual spa at home, all these tasks become your responsibility. You must ensure that all the rooms you are using are fully prepared, welcoming, tranquil and clean, and that they provide a suitable environment. You need to stock up on sufficient food and drink to last the duration of your retreat. You also require suitable clothing and other supplies, which are listed in detail in this section. These practical considerations will take some time to organize.

how much time can you devote?

Before considering the practicalities, the best place to start your preparations is with the central question: how many days do you want your retreat to last?

How much time you can devote to your spiritual spa needs careful thought. If you have never done a retreat before, then it is best to start with a basic one-day retreat. Although the retreat itself will only last a day, you need to devote one day (and possibly even two) beforehand to completing all the necessary preparations.

If you have decided to do a two- or three-day retreat, you also need to plan which schedule you will do on each day. For instance:

- A two-day retreat might comprise the basic one-day schedule (see page 10) followed by the classic one-day schedule (see page 11).

- A three-day retreat might consist of the basic one-day schedule, followed by the classic one-day schedule and finishing with a repeat of the basic one on the last day.

- A two- or three-day retreat will require up to two days' preparation – so you will need to devote five days to it in total.

freeing up time

Booking enough time off work may need to be planned well ahead of your actual retreat. You might just about manage to prepare and do a one-day retreat over a weekend, but taking one of the days as holiday would work much more successfully. For example, if you have Friday off work to make

Remember to note the dates of your spiritual spa in your diary and set these days aside for calm meditation.

While it may be necessary to book time off work it is not always a good idea to discuss your plans with colleagues.

preparations, you can do the retreat on the Saturday, and still have Sunday on which to rest or catch up on domestic chores, before returning to work on Monday.

When you book your time off work, it is probably best to keep your plans to yourself, unless you know your work colleagues well and believe they will be supportive of your planned retreat. Although you have a deep interest in the calm relaxation, rejuvenation and spiritual benefits of creating a sanctuary at home, not everyone will be sympathetic or open to the idea. Some people might even feel threatened by the concept, or think you are odd to contemplate such a thing.

creating space for yourself

Once you have booked your time off work, the next consideration is your family, or the people with whom you live or share rooms. If you live alone, then your home is already a private space. If you live with other people, you need to work out a way of creating your own private area for the duration of

Spend time with your partner before you begin your
spiritual spa and discuss any concerns they may have.

the retreat. The best solution is if your partner, family or friends can plan to be away. If this is not possible, then you must explain to them the necessity of having your own quiet, private space for as long as your spiritual spa lasts.

If your housemate is going to have to accommodate your need for silence, peace and privacy, then it is helpful to offer something in return. You could propose a similar quiet day for your housemate, or perhaps suggest that you wash the dishes for a week or spring-clean your shared accommodation. Whatever you decide, it is important that your housemate feels adequately compensated, so that he or she will take seriously (and respect) your need for privacy and silence, thus allowing you physical and mental space.

seeking your partner's support

If you live with your partner, it is important to discuss thoroughly the reasons why you are doing a retreat, and exactly how long it will take. If your partner understands your desire to meditate and rejuvenate, he or she will be much more accommodating of your need for a temporary separation and will not feel rejected or threatened in any way. Because your spiritual sanctuary must be experienced in silence, with no conversation at all, you need complete solitude. So on your actual retreat days you will not be able to see or communicate with your partner.

It is a good idea to spend some intimate time with your partner both before and after your retreat. This should make it clear that you love and care for him or her, and simply want some time alone for spiritual practice. If your partner has any concerns about why you are doing this, you need to have plenty of time to discuss this beforehand – and afterwards, if necessary. Silent, distant but loving support from your partner can contribute to the sense of peace and well-being that you will hopefully experience.

seeking family support

Being a parent of young children can pose particular problems, and if the children are extremely young, it is probably better to wait a year or two before undertaking a home retreat. If your children are old enough to accept that Mummy or Daddy wants to spend some time alone meditating quietly, then doing a short home retreat need not be a problem. You should plan for a loving carer to look after the children for the duration of your spiritual spa – someone whom they know well and trust.

Your children need to understand that you love them deeply and are not in any way rejecting them. A careful explanation of exactly what a home retreat is – and the opportunity for them to ask as many questions as they wish – should help to allay their concerns. As with your partner, it is good to plan to spend some special, intimate time with your children before and after the event.

To help your children feel involved, tell them all about your home retreat and explain what it entails.

what do you need?

Once you have worked out how long your spiritual spa is going last, and how many days of preparation it requires, you can book any time off from work and write the dates in your diary.

This makes it seem real, because you have now gone beyond the theoretical stage. The next thing you must do is to work out exactly – and in precise detail – everything (however small or insignificant) that you think you will need during your retreat.

The best method is to write a list of all your requirements. Start doing this well before the start date of your retreat, and keep the list close to hand. You will remember little things from time to time and should note them down before you forget them.

schedule

First, you need to write down your retreat schedule, detailing each activity throughout the day. You can use one of the two suggested schedules given on pages 10–11, or both of them, if your retreat will last longer than one day. Alternatively, you can use these schedules as a basis for creating your own, personalized schedule. This option gives you the freedom to create a schedule for a spiritual spa that really suits you and your needs, and that reflects what you want to achieve from it.

Once you have your schedule written down, work out exactly what supplies you will need during your retreat – from food and drink to essential oils. It's a good idea to create different categories of requirements to keep things in order – some suggestions for each category are given in the pages that follow.

Eat a healthy diet, including lots of fresh fruit, to cleanse and nourish the body during your spiritual spa.

Be creative and have some fun making up your own
recipes for special herbal tea blends.

food and drink

Because shopping for food (or eating outside your home) is not permitted during your home retreat, you must buy in beforehand all the food and drink you will need. This may not be as simple as it sounds. Ask yourself if you are the kind of person who often runs out of milk or bread, and then pops out to the local shop for basic items on a regular basis. If this sounds like your usual behaviour, then you need to plan your shopping very carefully and write down a list of exactly what food and drink you will need – and how much of each item.

Suggested meals and drinks for each stage of your spiritual spa are listed in the relevant programmes, together with the reasons for these particular choices and the benefits of consuming them. At this stage you just need to make a list of all the ingredients from the recipes for the three meals each day, noting down also any herbal teas and other suggested drinks. If you are unfamiliar with some of the ingredients, you may need to try a few different shops before locating exactly what you need, but a good health-food shop should stock many of the items.

clothing

For meditation and for yoga, stretching exercises and chi kung, you need loose-fitting (preferably stretchy) clothing that is comfortable to wear for long periods and allows for ease of movement. Because you will not wear shoes for either your meditation or your exercises, you also need a good pair of socks or soft-soled indoor shoes. Even in summer you require warm clothes for meditation, because the body is not moving (except slowly during walking meditation). People who meditate regularly often find that a large, warm shawl is especially useful. You can wrap the shawl around your shoulders to create a tent-like effect around your entire sitting body, including your feet (which, even with socks on, have a tendency to get cold).

bath and shower essentials

The early morning shower and evening bath require the use of different essential oils: stimulating, refreshing, detoxifying and uplifting essential oils in the morning shower; calming, soothing, purifying and relaxing essential oils in the evening bath. Essential oils can be expensive, but you don't need to buy a lot of different oils. A range of four or six basic essential oils will be sufficient, if you choose them carefully. For skin brushing, you will need a skin brush with a long handle so that you can reach right down your back, and with soft bristles that gently remove dead skin cells and stimulate the blood and lymphatic circulation.

other supplies

You will need some, or all, of the following items:

- A yoga mat is ideal for doing the yoga exercises on, but is not essential, because the easy yoga exercises recommended for a home retreat can be done comfortably on a carpeted floor.

Creating a home altar provides you with a dedicated place to make offerings and connect with spiritual energies.

- A meditation floor cushion, a specially designed meditation stool or a hard-backed chair is required for the sitting meditation.

- For the preparation of your sacred space or sanctuary, you ideally need a singing bowl or *ting-sha* Tibetan hand cymbals (see pages 36–37); however, if you don't have either of these items, substitute a simple ritual using incense, essential oils in a burner or room spray, candles, crystals, mirrors and lights.

- An inspiring sacred icon (such as a statue of Mary, Jesus, Shiva, Buddha or another deity) is needed for your altar.

- Fresh flowers and house plants contribute to making a pleasant retreat atmosphere.

- Prayer beads are recommended for reciting prayers and mantras.

- A journal is required for writing down your aims, commitments and your reflections and feelings.

- Suitable music is necessary if you choose to do the free dance exercise.

- An alarm clock is required to time your meditation sessions.

You will find simple, illustrated instructions for all the yoga, t'ai chi and other exercises in this book, so you don't need any other instruction manuals.

Vaporize essential oils in a burner as part of a simple ritual to prepare your sacred space.

making a personal commitment

Once all the material and physical requirements for your spiritual spa have been sorted out, it is time to make a formal commitment to your undertaking.

A contract of personal commitment to doing your home retreat can be an important preliminary step to success.

Doing this requires considerable reflection on the reasons why you have chosen to do a retreat. So it is beneficial to create a document – a contract of personal commitment to completing your home retreat – containing all your reasons for wishing to do it, and including all your hopes, anxieties, expectations and what you ultimately wish to achieve from it.

drawing up a contract

Writing a document like this may seem rather formal and 'over the top' – perhaps even unnecessary. You may think that once you have decided to create your spiritual spa, it is enough just to go ahead and do it. But a silent retreat composed largely of meditation is not in fact as easy as it sounds. When you sit in meditation, 'stuff' – emotions, feelings, memories and sensations – comes up from the deeper recesses of your mind and arises in your consciousness and your present awareness. These feelings and memories are not always pleasant or comfortable, and the temptation to abandon your meditation and do something else can be quite persuasive.

Perhaps you have done a meditation retreat before at a retreat centre, which will have given you a good and useful experience of meditation, and a realistic idea of what to expect from meditating at home. However, a retreat centre is geared towards facilitating people to meditate. There is a lot of silent, invisible support to help you through your retreat, as well as meditation teachers to talk matters through with you, if you experience any difficulties or if your determination to complete the retreat wanes. When you create a retreat sanctuary

Sit down comfortably and take time to reflect upon your reasons for wanting to undertake a home retreat.

at home, you need to generate all your own determination and you must support yourself. Drawing up and signing a contract beforehand is part of your support system.

If you have not meditated before, you may be feeling a bit nervous at this stage, and may be wondering if you can manage even a one-day retreat at home by yourself. However, there is nothing to worry about, if you prepare yourself adequately beforehand. Once you are quite clear about your motivation, you can find within yourself all the inner resolve needed to complete your first one- or even two-day home retreat. Composing

Sitting meditation helps you relax mind, body and spirit, letting go of mental and physical stress in the process.

your own personal contract and signing it will give you an important incentive to help you successfully finish your home retreat.

what do you hope to achieve?

Reflecting on this question, and discovering some answers, is a good way to start writing out your contract. There are some fairly general answers to this question, and most people would say that in the first instance they want to feel relaxed, peaceful and rejuvenated. These aims are a good beginning, but you can explore your motivation for doing a home retreat in greater depth. Some more profound reasons are explored below.

Stress-related illness is an unfortunate, but increasingly common, phenomenon of modern life. The chances of suffering a heart attack or a stroke have increased significantly alongside the speedy pace of contemporary day-to-day living. Cancer and other life-threatening illnesses are not scientifically proven to be caused by stress, but stress may well play a role in many diseases. Sitting meditation, healthy eating, detoxifying the body and physical meditation movements such as t'ai chi and yoga, all help the body to de-stress, relax and heal itself. One great benefit of doing a home retreat regularly is restoring health and harmony to your mind, body and spirit.

Although we are called 'human beings', we in fact spend most of our lives *doing* something or other, rather than just *being*. A spiritual spa gives you the opportunity to simply *be*; there are no pressures to do anything other than sitting meditation, movement meditation and caring for your body. There is a real joy and peace to be found in not doing anything other than looking after

Light candles on your altar to help create a suitable atmosphere for meditation.

yourself and simply being. During a home retreat you can be at one with yourself; you have the chance to discover who you really are beneath the superficial activities of daily life.

Scientists are endlessly fascinated with exploring external phenomena; divers want to explore deep oceans, and mountaineers feel compelled to climb high peaks, simply because they are there. When you meditate you embark on an equally fascinating journey, looking into the depths and breadths of your own mind. What is the mind? We normally take our minds for granted – we think, without realizing that we are thinking. Daily life offers very few opportunities to become familiar with the way the mind actually functions. But a meditatory retreat involves an inner voyage of discovery, offering a precious opportunity to explore your own mind.

setting out your contract

The main item to include in your contract is a statement of your personal commitment to complete the home retreat exactly – or as nearly as possible – as described in the schedule. You need to take your commitment seriously, but it should not be a burden to you in any way. After all, you have the freedom to personalize your schedule to suit yourself (although it should be based on one of the two schedules suggested on pages 10–11). A spiritual spa is something you have freely chosen to undertake: something you wish to do. So your personal contract is there to help you keep going if you feel lazy, or want to cheat on the schedule, or succumb to negative thoughts during your meditation sessions.

To make your statement of personal commitment, write down a sentence or two describing your resolve. It is important to have belief in yourself, so write down another couple of sentences that reflect your trust in yourself. Underneath, list all your objectives, aims and expectations for the retreat. You can also include any worries, doubts and anxieties that you might have. At the end of the retreat you can review your contract and see how many aims were realized, and whether any of your doubts were justified. Finally, sign your name at the end of the contract, leaving a little space above your signature, in case you wish to add anything to what you have already written.

silence and boundaries

The necessity of silence in your home has already been mentioned, but needs a little more explanation. You might ask why your retreat needs to be done in complete silence. Silence enables the meditating mind to begin to settle down and let go of any distractions that arise from the stimulus of sound, such as talking and listening to music and the words of songs. Not reading anything other than the instructions on how to do yoga, t'ai chi and other exercises is also an important aspect of silence for the mind.

Modern life does not create many opportunities for silence, unless you live somewhere deeply rural, so being on your own in total silence may feel strange at first. You will start to notice every tiny external sound: the central heating boiler, floorboards creaking and birds singing. At first these noises will seem strangely fascinating, but this is simply your mind coming to terms with an unusually long absence of major sounds. Once you have adjusted to the silence, you will begin to realize the benefits for your meditation – such as being able to develop a calm attentiveness.

In the following section you will read about creating a sacred space (and the accompanying boundaries) in the room in which you will undertake your home-retreat activities. This will explain the more subtle aspects of boundaries. The boundaries referred to here mean ensuring that no one enters your space while you are undertaking your spiritual spa. The presence of another person will distract you, and will entice you away from the silent concentration you have developed. So it is vital that you make firm boundaries between yourself and others, and that these are respected (if you share your home with other people and they are unable to be away).

common questions

In order to meditate, do I need to be a religious person or belong to a particular faith?

You do not need to be an adherent of any religion to meditate. Meditation is a spiritual practice common to most religious traditions, but all meditative practices share the principle of the mind becoming familiar with the different aspects of itself. However, if you are a religious person and follow a particular doctrine, then meditation can consolidate your faith. There are particular meditations specific to each religion. The basic techniques suggested in this book are drawn mostly from the various Buddhist traditions.

Do I need any special qualities to be able to meditate?

You do not require any special qualities in order to meditate. Although previous meditation experience is useful, it is by no means essential. Anyone who has the wish to meditate can do so by following the step-by-step instructions given in this book.

Do I need to have any previous experience of yoga or chi kung to do the exercises?

The various exercises included in the two schedules are explained clearly, with step-by-step instructions: they are all easy yoga stretches and poses, chi kung exercises or t'ai chi movements. Any healthy person can safely undertake them. Some of the simple stretches and movements are simplified variations, drawn from one or other of these traditions. They are included as basic movements to do between sitting meditation sessions, as the body can become a little stiff or tense, and stretching and other movements are helpful to avoid pain or cramps developing.

Remember to wear comfortable clothes that allow easy movement for doing yoga and chi kung exercises.

pre-retreat preparations

The evening and night before you begin give you further time to prepare yourself mentally and psychologically to start your home retreat.

At this stage you will have assembled everything of a practical nature that you need for the retreat, and will have written out your contract and your daily schedule (or different schedules for each day, if your retreat is going to last for several days). However, you probably still need some time for final inner preparation.

Before your retreat starts, spend a quiet, relaxing evening at home in a calm atmosphere.

Most meditation centres actually start their retreats at 17.00 or 18.00 on the first evening, and the retreat boundaries and silence begin from that point. Although there are probably only two or three meditation sessions that evening, these are good psychological preparation for the following morning, because when you wake up you have already begun the retreat and are in the right frame of mind to meditate all day.

For a home retreat lasting just a day (or a few days), you don't need to start it the evening before. You should spend a calm evening – ideally alone and silent – so you can begin to reflect upon what you will be doing for the next day or so during the retreat. Try not to watch television, listen to music or read novels and magazines, although a little reading about meditation can be inspirational.

You should eat a light (preferably vegetarian) evening meal, and try to eat no later than 19.00. Avoid drinking any alcohol, black tea or coffee, and if you are a smoker – if this is at all possible for you – stop smoking now until the end of the retreat. Have an early night and go to bed no later than 22.00. You need to remember to set your alarm clock according to the time at which your schedule will start the following morning.

Go to bed early, remembering to set your alarm for the early call that signals the start of your retreat.

Getting a good night's sleep will ensure you wake energised and ready to spend the day in calm meditation.

overcoming doubts and nerves

During your quiet pre-retreat evening you will have time to reflect on your reasons for creating a spiritual spa, and to mentally reconfirm your intention to complete your home retreat properly. It is only natural to experience doubts and anxieties, and you may even feel some resistance towards doing the retreat and start to wonder why you thought you wanted to do it in the first place. If this happens, let these thoughts or doubts arise and pass; they are not a real indication that you have changed your mind.

When you are about to embark on something unusual, different and a little challenging, such as meditation and the other home-retreat activities, the mind can create illusory obstacles. This is because the mind finds it easier to stay with the familiar and the known, rather than trying something new and different. Usually, when you have time off work and are free of all social and family commitments, you can spend your time lying in bed or doing whatever you choose. If you feel your determination faltering, read through your contract. You wrote and signed it because you really *wanted* to undertake a home retreat.

On the other hand you may be feeling really excited about doing a retreat, and longing for the morning to come, so that you can make a start.

benefits of an early start

Almost all meditation centres begin each day early in the morning, and some start very early indeed: at 03.00 or 04.00. Starting at this hour may seem intimidating or unnecessary, and you might wonder why it is a good idea to begin each day so early.

Getting up out of a warm, cosy bed on a cold, dark morning does not sound particularly appealing. However, for serious and experienced meditators, the early-morning start reflects their determination to meditate. Getting up really early can be seen as a challenge – a test of your resolve to make the most of each day you have the opportunity to practise meditation.

Once you have some experience of meditation, learning how to extend yourself a little more on each retreat can be a useful way to progress with your meditation practice. It is not uncommon in retreat centres to see people getting up even earlier than the schedule indicates, in order to spend as much time as possible in meditation. However, such enthusiasm must be balanced by a realistic appraisal of your meditation capabilities. If you push yourself too hard at the beginning, you might 'burn out' and over-extend yourself, and perhaps feel unable to complete the retreat.

getting the balance right

You may have noticed that for home retreats lasting a few days, the suggested schedules start and finish, whenever possible, with an easier day. Arranging your time like this means that you start with a basic one-day schedule and gradually work up to the longer and harder classic one-day schedule. This prevents you from over-extending yourself at the outset, and allows you to settle into your meditation practice before embarking on the more complex schedule. And making the last day an easier one gives you some time in which to relax a little and psychologically adjust to finishing the retreat. Then, when you resume normal life the following day, the transition will not be too abrupt.

Taking care of yourself in this way during a home retreat gives you the best chance of making the most of your meditation practice: providing enough of a challenge, but not pushing you too hard. If your experience of meditation is a positive one, you will probably wish to try another retreat at a later time; if you overdo things when you first start meditating, you run the risk of creating a negative experience, which may put you off wanting to meditate again.

Even if getting out of your warm bed first thing seems offputting, once you have done it, the experience will alter your feelings. Early morning is a special time of day: the mind is fresh and clear, and this is a wonderful time to meditate. Witnessing the light gradually breaking through the dark at dawn is a powerful and magical experience, so it is well worth making the effort to get up early during your home retreat.

The early morning is a special time of day, and getting up then allows you to enjoy its benefits.

creating a private sanctuary

In order for your home retreat to be effective, you need to create a private sanctuary where you will be undisturbed. This has two aspects: making the space private from outside interference, and creating a sacred space so that whenever you enter your sanctuary, you feel inspired to focus solely on your retreat activities. It is worth spending time and effort setting up your sanctuary as thoroughly as you can, because this will be beneficial for your retreat. This preparation also helps you develop the right frame of mind to undertake the activities.

When choosing the physical space for your sanctuary, check for potentially adverse outside influences. Make sure there will not be too much noise from traffic, machinery, people, music, and so on. The ideal room is spacious, uncluttered and has a large window for natural light. This provides a good basic area in which to create your sanctuary: a sacred space for your home retreat.

sacred space

Once you have decided which room to use for your home retreat, the first thing to do is to clean it thoroughly and empty it as much as possible, because a clean, empty space facilitates inner spaciousness and peace of mind.

Create your sacred space using lighted candles, which are also suitable for a simple purification ritual.

Bring into your chosen room the cushion or chair on which you plan to meditate, and a yoga mat if you have one.

This room will be transformed into your dedicated retreat space, your sanctuary and refuge from mundane life and daily activities. When you are in this room you will be sitting in meditation, doing movement meditation, stretches or one of the other retreat activities. You should not eat or drink in this room, or even bring food or drink into your sacred space.

Before doing one of the rituals described below to make the space sacred, you need to purify the room of old, negative or mundane psychic energies. You can either use a burner to vaporize essential oils or a room spray, although a burner creates a more powerful purifying effect. To prepare a burner, place a tea-light in the lower aperture, then light the candle. Half-fill the upper bowl with water,

and sprinkle on eight to ten drops of essential oils. To prepare a room spray, put up to 60 drops of essential oils into a 100 ml (3½ fl oz) bottle of water with an atomizer, then spray the room thoroughly from top to bottom.

choosing a ritual

Once the room is clean, relatively empty and purified, you can perform one of the rituals described below to create your sacred space. These rituals not only empower and sanctify the room; they also help to create definite boundaries. Whenever you take breaks from your retreat activities, you physically and mentally leave the sacred space in order to rest, eat, sleep, and so on. Maintaining strict boundaries in this way keeps the space dedicated to spiritual, peaceful activities, untainted by worldly concerns.

Before entering the room to perform any of these rituals, take off your shoes – and make sure you always remove your shoes before entering the room from now on, until the end of your home retreat. This is a fundamental principle for maintaining sacred spaces, and keeps the place both physically and psychically clean and pure. It explains why you remove your shoes before entering temples and meditation rooms in many religious traditions. Once you are inside the room, close the door mindfully. As you do so, be aware that all areas inside the room belong to the sacred space, and that this space is now separated from all areas outside the room.

purifying essential oils

- Traditional essential oils for purification, and to help create a sacred space, include juniper, frankincense, pine, cedarwood, lemon, cypress, myrrh, elemi and sandalwood.

- Other, more readily available essential oils, such as rosemary, lavender, orange and geranium, may also be used.

- All essential oils are purifying to a greater or lesser extent, and choosing those that appeal to you will also be effective.

Walking slowly round the room ringing ting-sha *bells is a lovely way to create a sacred space.*

ritual using *ting-sha* bells

One ritual to create your sacred space involves using *ting-sha* bells, and – in common with all these simple rituals – some incense and candles.

Ting-sha bells are small Tibetan hand cymbals, joined by a string or leather thong. When one cymbal is struck against the other, a haunting, mellifluous sound resonates from them. The traditional purpose of *ting-sha* bells was to summon: they ring out to make us aware in the here and now, to be present to whatever is happening in our minds and bodies and our immediate environment. In this way they are a useful aid to meditation.

The penetrating reverberations of the *ting-sha* are also used to summon spirits from the ethereal realms beyond human consciousness. Traditionally they were used in guidance prayers, together with burned food offerings for the dead, or to appease the tormented spirits known as 'hungry ghosts'. However, they can also be effectively used in the context of creating a sacred space and psychically cleansing the atmosphere of your room.

1 Light four candles and some incense. Place a candle in each corner of the room. Place the lighted incense in an incense holder, and put this in the middle of the room.

2 Walk round the room slowly, ringing the *ting-sha* bells together with a slow, steady rhythm as you go.

3 Sit quietly and meditate on your reasons for doing your home retreat. Mentally renew your commitment to complete your retreat, even if difficulties arise. Then mentally request the universal divine energies – or the gods, goddesses or spirits of your choice – to consecrate your sacred space.

4 Continue to ring the *ting-sha* bells for a few minutes to purify and bless the room, and to dedicate the space to your home retreat.

ritual using a singing bowl

The sound of a singing bowl is just as resonant and ethereal as that of the *ting-sha* bells. Singing bowls are also Tibetan, and their haunting sound is equally effective in rituals for creating a sacred space.

Traditional singing bowls are of a medium size and are made of metal. Their singing sound is created by firmly holding a short, thick wooden stick on the outer rim of the bowl, then moving it round repeatedly until a singing sound starts to emanate from the bowl.

1 Light four candles and some incense. Place a candle in each corner of the room. Place the lighted incense in an incense holder, and put this in the middle of the room.

2 Sound the singing bowl as you walk slowly round the room.

3 Complete the ritual in the same manner as described opposite, sounding the singing bowl again at the end to dedicate your sacred space.

feng shui rituals

Feng shui originated in around 4000 BCE, and is the ancient Chinese art of organizing the space in your home in the best way to promote health, happiness and success. It is based on the Chinese principle of natural energy, known as *chi*. *Chi* can be described as the feel and atmosphere of a room, and how easily the flow of energy moves between the different areas. Amending this, according to the principles of feng shui, can improve the energy of your room and help to make it a harmonious sacred space in which to meditate.

- Use mirrors to create the illusion of space in irregular-shaped or small rooms. This corrects any awkward feeling and harmonizes the flow of *chi* in the room.

- Use lights or candles to activate the flow of *chi* in corners, which might otherwise stagnate.

- Put plants in front of corners to create a living, vibrant energy. Bushy plants help to slow down *chi*, and are useful placed near the door.

- Light candles to add fire and warmth to a room. They are particularly recommended for rooms facing north-east.

- If possible, use a north-facing room, because in feng shui this is associated with meditation and solitary creativity, so it is an ideal choice for a home retreat.

Sound the singing bowl as you move around your chosen space in preparation for the meditation sessions.

home altar

Your sacred space is incomplete without an altar on which to focus all your spiritual energy and make offerings to divine energies or gods.

creating an altar

Once you have purified your room and performed one of the rituals described on pages 36–37, the final step in creating a sacred space is to set up your altar. This provides a dedicated place to make offerings to the divine energies or gods. Even if you have secular tendencies, a plain altar containing simple offerings gives you the opportunity to connect with higher spiritual energies, creating a suitable mood for the meditations and rutuals you will undertake during your spiritual spa activities.

A suitable altar can be created on a small table, a mantelpiece or a shelf. If the surface is made of an aesthetically pleasing material, such as wood or marble, clean and polish it thoroughly; if the surface is unattractive (or if you simply prefer) cover it with a beautiful cloth, such as a silk or cotton scarf or a piece of embroidered material.

choosing suitable objects

The objects that you place on your altar need not be complex or ornate – simplicity can be more spiritually authentic than a cluster of muddled objects. What is important is that the items you choose hold spiritual significance for you, and in this way act as a symbol of your spiritual practice. It is a good idea to select one central image that you find inspiring and beautiful to look at and to which you can direct your focus during your retreat session.

- If you are Christian, then a cross, or a statue or picture of Jesus, Mary or another Christian saint, would be appropriate.

- A Jewish person might choose a Star of David.

- A Hindu might select a statue or picture of Shiva, Brahma, Vishnu or some other Hindu deity.

- A Buddhist might choose a statue or picture of Buddha, or perhaps a photograph of the Dalai Lama or another leading Buddhist teacher.

- If you do not follow any religion, you could choose a large, beautiful crystal, or any other object that you regard as a source of spiritual wisdom.

Whatever spiritual symbol you choose, place your icon in the centre of your altar. During your home retreat you can make offerings on the altar. These offerings are not being made to the icon you have chosen – their purpose is to connect with and honour your own spiritual potential for universal love, wisdom, compassion and other enlightened qualities, as symbolized by your chosen icon.

Fill a shallow bowl with fresh rose petals, slightly moistened, as an alternative to a vase of fresh flowers.

making offerings

Traditional offerings include:

- Burning incense or, if you prefer, you can vaporize essential oils in a burner. Both incense and essential oils create a tranquil, spiritual atmosphere that is conducive to meditation.

- Lighting a candle, or several candles, adds to this atmosphere.

- A bowl of water (or a few small bowls) makes an appropriate offering and symbolizes spiritual purity.

- A small vase of fresh flowers provides a connection with Nature, and symbolizes the impermanence of all living things.

To renew your spiritual commitment for each of your meditation sessions, it is important to refresh the offerings each time you sit down to meditate. These preliminaries serve to remind you of your purpose, and are an integral and important aspect of spiritual practice. Before each meditation session, light a stick of incense, or top up your burner with essential oils and light the tea-light. Renew the bowl with fresh water, and light the candles. Keeping your altar clean and tidy shows respect for the divine energies or gods. At the conclusion of your meditation, extinguish the candles and remove the spent stick of incense, or clean out the essential oil burner.

✦ basic early-morning schedule

08.00 get up and shower, after using a natural exfoliating body scrub with essential oils

08.30 drink a glass of hot water with freshly squeezed lemon juice to stimulate and detoxify the liver

08.45 simple stretching exercises

09.00 calm meditation

09.30 breakfast of fruit, yogurt and muesli, with a cup of herbal tea

✳ classic early-morning schedule

06.30 get up and shower, after using a natural exfoliating body scrub with essential oils

07.00 drink a glass of hot water with freshly squeezed lemon juice to stimulate and detoxify the liver

07.15 Salutation to the Dawn yoga exercise

07.30 calm meditation

08.00 breakfast of fruit, yogurt and muesli, with a cup of herbal tea

basic activities are indicated by ✦
classic activities are indicated by ✳

early-morning programme

Assuming that you have completed all your preparations as set out in the Introduction and in Preparing for a Retreat, you are by now ready to start the first day of your spiritual spa. During your preparations you will probably have experienced a mood shift, and should be starting to feel just about ready to embark on your first home-retreat day. It is, however, quite usual to feel a little apprehensive and nervous beforehand, and you should not let this put you off beginning the retreat.

✦✱ exfoliate your body

The first activity of the day is giving yourself an exfoliating body scrub. This removes dead skin cells and leaves your skin feeling soft and invigorated, glowing and sweet-smelling from the essential oils.

This is a rejuvenating treatment for your skin based on an Indian body scrub. It is usually done by a massage therapist, beautician, family member or friend, who scrubs you all over with a traditional mixture of finely ground grains, fruit peel, spices and aromatic oils. However, the scrub is easy enough to do for yourself and makes an invigorating start to your home retreat.

The recipe opposite has been adapted from the traditional one to make it easy to use. You need to prepare the dried orange peel a few days beforehand: one large orange will make enough dried peel for the recipe. Using a paring knife, strip off fine segments of orange peel, making sure that you leave all the white pith behind on the fruit. Spread the peel strips out on a piece of paper to dry, which will take two or three days to complete. Once you are sure the peel is quite dry, use a clean coffee or breadcrumb grinder to pulverize it, and then store the peel crumbs in an airtight jar.

You can mix up all the dry ingredients the night before, if you prefer not to do this first thing in the morning; and then simply add the essential oils and water just before you want to do the scrub. The oils suggested here are luxurious and traditional choices, but you can use any essential oil whose fragrance you enjoy. It is best to apply the body scrub standing in a bath or shower cubicle, or on a mat, newspaper or towel, because it is quite a messy procedure.

As you apply the mixture to your body, remember that this early-morning ritual forms part

Choose a bowl that is large enough to comfortably scoop out handfuls of body scrub.

Applying the scrub to your body mindfully and with awareness is very similar to meditation.

rejuvenating scrub

ingredients

2 tablespoons fine oatmeal

2 tablespoons ground almonds

1 teaspoon dried, finely ground orange peel

1 teaspoon rosehip granules

5 drops in total of rose, jasmine, sandalwood or
other essential oil of your choice

1 Place all the dry ingredients in a medium-sized bowl and mix thoroughly.

2 Add the essential oil, together with a little warm water to make a fine, crumbly mixture. Don't use too much water or you will end up with a sticky mess.

body scrub ritual

1 Stand in the bath or shower, or on a towel or mat spread on the floor. Taking small handfuls of the body scrub, rub yourself vigorously with small circular movements all over your body. Be systematic and mindful so that you don't forget any parts of your body. It is a good idea to do your legs and arms first because they are the easiest to cover, and then as much of the rest of your body as you can reach.

2 The scrub dries quickly, and most of it will fall straight off your body. When you have finished, lightly brush off any leftover crumbs. You are now ready to take a shower.

of your home retreat, and bring your full attention to the task at hand. Really feel the effect of what you are doing to your skin and underlying tissues; be focused and aware as you rub the scrub all over your skin. Try to avoid daydreaming, or thinking about anything other than what you are doing at the present moment. Don't be tempted to break the silence by humming or singing – even though you may find this difficult, if your usual habit is to listen to the radio first thing in the morning.

✦✶ purifying shower

Although taking a shower is a usual everyday activity, during a home retreat it is transformed into a ritual by bringing conscious intent, awareness and attention to what you are doing.

A shower can become a substantially enriched experience simply by taking time to think about why and how you are doing it, and by reflecting upon your experience. Making your shower into a cleansing ritual can transform this mundane experience into a spiritual one.

Think about your normal morning shower and how you usually experience it. Perhaps you stumble out of bed, half-asleep, turn on the shower and wait impatiently for the water to heat up. Clambering into the shower, you wash perfunctorily – largely unaware of what you are doing, not taking time to enjoy the shower, and thinking about what you will be doing later that day rather than being here and now in the present moment. Does this scenario sound familiar?

During a home retreat you will transform your morning shower into a nurturing ritual that prepares you – mind, body and spirit – for meditation. The common perception of taking a shower is simply that it is a means to wash and get clean. But another way to regard the shower is as a morning ritual, washing away the detritus of sleep and awakening yourself to

the new day. Being present to the whole experience, rather than taking it for granted, gives the mind an insight into what it means to shower. For example, as you pay full attention to the drops of water raining down freely over your body, you may intuitively realize that you are incredibly fortunate to be able to have this experience.

Many people in the world – in fact, the majority of the world's population – are unable to enjoy a similar experience; they may not live with running water in their homes, or even have access to clean drinking water. Your morning shower that you take for granted would be an unbelievable luxury to such people. An insight like this makes you aware of how lucky you are. It should not make you feel guilty, although if it prompts you to give a little money to charities that help people receive clean water, then this is a compassionate response to the world situation. Rather, such insights should help you appreciate your own good fortune and not take anything for granted. So take a little time to deeply enjoy your morning shower, without guilt, but with increased awareness.

Try using uplifting, stimulating essential oils in your morning shower to refresh mind, body and spirit.

early-morning essential oils

You can use uplifting, stimulating essential oils in your morning shower to wake you up and freshen your mind and body, if you choose.

- Rosemary, geranium, lemon, peppermint and juniper are suitable choices (but use only 3–4 drops if you choose peppermint, as this is a very powerful-smelling essential oil).

- A particularly nice blend to use is 3 drops of rosemary and 4 drops of geranium, but feel free to experiment with essential oils of your choice.

shower ritual

1 Just before you get into the shower, sprinkle 6–8 drops of your chosen essential oil onto the floor. As the hot water vaporizes the oil, you will gradually become enveloped in a cloud of fragrant steam.

2 During your shower the water will wash off any last traces of the body scrub. However, as you have already exfoliated and removed any dead skin cells, there is no need to scrub down with soap. In fact it feels much nicer simply to let the water pour over your already cleansed and exfoliated skin, and to wash just those parts of your body that you need to, for hygiene purposes.

3 Take your time in the shower, without being unduly wasteful of the precious resource of water, to enjoy the sensation of water pouring onto your body. Mentally be aware of each part of your body, checking out how it feels. If you find any areas of tension, try to relax them consciously.

4 Breathe in the fragrance of the vaporized essential oils, and imagine them entering your body through your lungs and skin. Then visualize the particles of essential oils travelling around your bloodstream, bringing healing relaxation to all the different parts of your body. Really feel the effect of the essential oils and the hot water on your entire body.

5 After your shower, dry yourself mindfully and get dressed, ready to continue with your home retreat.

✦ simple stretching exercises

These exercises help to loosen and stretch your muscles before you sit for your first meditation session. They should be done slowly and thoughtfully, which helps to ensure that you do not pull or strain any muscles.

These stretches also help you to become aware of your body as you use all the different muscles and joints. In this way they are grounding and help you to be fully in – and conscious of – your body, which is a good way to prepare for sitting meditation.

When you have been sitting still in meditation for some time, it is important to ease the muscles gently before moving on – especially if you will be doing more strenuous movements immediately afterwards. So you can also do a few of these stretches after each sitting meditation, if you wish. Before starting the stretches after sitting in meditation, stand up slowly, being aware of whether you have any tight or tense muscles from sitting still.

1 Stretch one arm upwards, downwards and then out to the side. Repeat this sequence a few times. Then shake the arm about, releasing and consciously letting go of all tension. Repeat with the other arm.

2 Standing on one leg, raise the other leg and clasp it to the front of your body. Hold this stretch for a few seconds, then stand on both feet. Repeat twice more with the same leg. Then, again standing on one leg, shake the other leg about, releasing all tension. Repeat the whole sequence with the other leg.

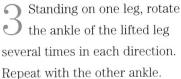

3 Standing on one leg, rotate the ankle of the lifted leg several times in each direction. Repeat with the other ankle.

4 Standing with your legs wide apart, raise your arms and lean over to one side. Hold for a few seconds, then return to the upright position. Then lean over to the other side. Repeat twice for each side.

5 Standing with your legs close together, lean over and touch your toes. Repeat a few times.

6 Standing with your feet slightly apart, slowly and gently rotate your head in a circle, first one way and then the other. Repeat a couple of times.

Be careful not to over-stretch or strain your neck muscles, but do stretch sufficiently to feel the release of any tension.

*salutation to the dawn

These poses are drawn from yoga, which means balance or equanimity. This is a physical meditation that ultimately leads towards enlightenment, and also cultivates a high level of physical fitness and mental and emotional calm.

1 Start by standing with feet together, and arms by your sides, palms loosely held against your thighs. Look straight ahead and hold your body upright and relaxed.

2 Inhale while you raise your arms out to the sides, palms facing upwards. Bend your knees slightly as you continue to raise your arms above your head, keeping them straight.

3 Continue inhaling as you raise your arms until they are stretched straight above your head, with the palms open and facing each other.

4 Exhale as you lean forward from the hips. Take your arms out to the sides at right angles from your body, and keep your head in a straight line with the rest of your spine.

5 Continue exhaling and pull in your stomach and abdomen as you bend over with your arms hanging down. If your body is flexible you may be able to hold your ankles and rest your head against your lower legs (as shown), but don't force any movement beyond your capability.

6 Inhale as you raise your upper body to make a right angle with the floor. Your back and neck should make a straight line. Keep your arms hanging down, feet flat on the floor and your legs straight.

7 As you slowly exhale, bend over from the hips and repeat the fifth asana.

8 As you inhale, bend your knees until you can put your hands flat on the floor. Then exhale and kneel first on your right leg and then your left, so that you end up kneeling on all fours.

9 Keeping the natural curve in your lower spine, pull in your stomach. Pull your shoulders away from your ears, release any tension and open your chest. Breathe naturally for a few breaths.

10 Exhale as you gently lower your buttocks downwards until they rest on your heels. Lean forward until your head touches the ground, then stretch your arms out in front of you.

11 Move one arm behind you. The palm should face upwards at first, then allow the fingers to relax into a natural cupping around the foot.

12 As you rest more heavily on your heels, move the other arm behind you, then relax and cup the other foot in the same way.

13 Bring your arms round in front of you as you inhale. Take the weight on to your arms as you lift your buttocks upwards to form a triangle with the floor. Keep your arms straight as you lift your heels off the floor, lengthening the ankles. Keeping your body weight evenly distributed between your fingers and heels of your hands, stretch upwards.

14 Bring your heels back to the floor as you exhale. Hold this asana for three or four breaths.

15 Now inhale and step forwards, placing your left leg between your hands. Lift your chest and look forwards and down.

16 As you finish breathing in, move the right leg forwards so that both feet are between your hands. Keep your knees bent and your stomach and abdomen drawn in.

17 Then, as you gradually exhale, move into the fifth asana again.

18 Inhale and move into the fourth asana. Bend your knees slightly as you move upwards to support your spine.

19 Continue the in breath and move into the third asana.

20 As you begin to exhale, bring your arms down and out to the sides so you are standing in the second asana.

21 Finally continue the exhalation and bring your arms down to your sides, as in the first asana. You then either repeat the sequence, or finish.

✦* calm meditation

You have now arrived at the point where you will be sitting the first meditation session. Calm meditation forms the basis of the other meditations you will practising during your retreat.

The technique is drawn from a Buddhist meditation traditionally known as 'tranquil abiding meditation'. Although the instructions are easy to follow, the method is profound and has been used for many centuries in different cultures to help the mind find peace and tranquillity. Calm meditation is suitable for beginners as well as for more experienced meditators, so it does not matter whether or not you have any previous meditation experience.

You can meditate sitting either on a cushion or a hard-backed chair. If you are an experienced meditator, you will know which of these options suits you best. If you have not meditated previously, have both a cushion and a chair in the room so that if you try sitting on a chair and it feels uncomfortable, you can simply switch to a cushion.

1 Either cross your legs and sit on the cushion on the floor, or sit upright on the chair with both feet on the floor. It is important to keep your back straight, and to be able to sit comfortably for as long as your meditation session lasts.

2 Set your alarm for 30 minutes, and then try to forget about the time. Sit in a relaxed posture, but remember to keep your back straight. Close or half-shut your eyes and place your hands in your lap.

3 Now bring your attention to your breathing, by becoming aware of the sensation at the tip of your nostrils as you inhale and exhale. Be aware of watching your breath without judging the process, and don't try to change how you breathe – just watch your breath.

4 This simple focus on your breathing puts you in touch with what it means to be alive. Becoming aware of the natural – almost tidal – rhythm of your breathing is calming and inspires tranquillity. Because breathing does not require conscious effort or control (your body breathes naturally, without you having to do anything), most of the time you are not really aware that you are breathing.

5 When your mind wanders off into your usual thoughts and feelings, gently bring your attention back to your breathing, but without judging or being hard on yourself. It is the nature of the mind for thoughts to arise, and you are used to letting your mind think freely during your ususal everyday activities, so you are unlikely to be able to maintain sustained awareness of your breathing for very long when you first start practising calm meditation. Gently

Practising calm meditation during your home retreat is a wonderful way to find inner peace and harmony.

return your attention to the breath, however many times your mind wanders off.

6 When your alarm rings, gently open your eyes and shift your position before getting up. Do a few simple stretches (see pages 46–47) if you feel any stiffness or tension in your body. Take a few minutes to reflect on your meditation session and to apreciate the time you have allowed yourself to spend in this tranquil state before slowly moving on to your next home-retreat activity.

food and drink

After your shower, it's time to prepare and drink a glass of hot water with the juice of half a freshly squeezed lemon added to it, then later a cup of refreshing and stimulating herbal tea.

A glass teapot with a drainer insert, like the one shown here, is a good alternative to a china teapot.

As you have started the day by giving yourself an invigorating body scrub, you have already begun to stimulate your various body systems. Hot water drunk first thing in the morning by itself stimulates the digestion, aiding elimination and the general healthy functioning of the digestive process. The addition of freshly squeezed lemon juice enhances this, and helps the liver to process and eliminate toxins. In fact, hot lemon is refreshing and quite palatable, once you become used to drinking it, and your body will really appreciate this healthy start to the day. You will feel ready to start doing your physical meditation exercises shortly after drinking the hot water and lemon.

herbal teas

After your first sitting meditation, it's time to make your breakfast. This is accompanied – or, preferably, followed – by a cup of herbal tea. It's a good idea to choose a herbal tea that is gently stimulating and refreshing for this time of the day.

Herbal teas are more correctly known as infusions or tisanes and there are quite a few to choose from, so you need to know a little bit about them. When you are shopping before your home retreat begins, try to buy organic herbal teas and to choose brands without extra flavourings and additives. It is surprising how many 'adulterated' herbal teas are on offer these days, in which the bulk of the ingredients are synthetic flavours, rather than pure herbs. You can purchase either loose herbal tea or herbal teabags. It's a good idea to experiment before your retreat starts with some of the different herbal teas, to establish which ones you find palatable and which ones you don't like.

early-morning teas

For your early morning drink you could try one of the following herbal teas: peppermint, spearmint, fennel, nettle, vervain or lemon balm.

- Peppermint is strong-tasting, stimulating and refreshing. It is also a good digestive, and is traditionally drunk after meals, especially in some Middle Eastern countries.

- Spearmint is similar, but is gentler and has a slight natural sweetness that distinguishes it from peppermint.

- Fennel is the most detoxifying of the herbal teas, although nettle also makes a good purifying tea.

- Vervain and lemon balm are gentle, calming and refreshing.

how to brew herbal tea

1 The best method of making herbal teas is in a china teapot dedicated solely to brewing herbal teas (not in a pot that is used to make black tea). Warm the pot, then put in your chosen herbal tea: either loose herbs or teabags.

2 Pour in sufficient boiling water, put on the lid, then leave the tea to infuse for a few minutes. Herbal infusions are best drunk hot, although they can be drunk lukewarm or even cold, if preferred.

3 Some people like to sweeten herbal teas. Organic honey is the best natural sweetener. So add one or two teaspoons, according to taste.

The word 'breakfast' actually means to break your fast from the previous night when you were asleep. This means that the body has not ingested any food for six to eight hours, or even longer, depending on when you ate your last meal. So, at the start of the day, it is important to eat sufficient healthy food to prepare yourself for meditation and the other home-retreat activities.

It is sometimes assumed that fasting is a good thing to do when you are undertaking a meditation retreat. However, this is only suitable for experienced meditators, who must follow specific guidelines to prevent them feeling faint and dizzy. Eating well during your home retreat is strongly recommended. Giving the body sufficient nutritious food helps to prevent you 'spacing out' during your meditation sessions, so that you can make the most of the experience.

Eating a nutritious, healthy breakfast is an excellent way to start the day.

breakfast foods

The old saying 'You are what you eat', is as relevant today as it has always been, and eating well is especially important when you are doing a home retreat. A healthy, nutritious diet leads to longevity and general well-being, and may help prevent many minor ailments and even more serious diseases. Although there is no guarantee that a balanced diet will prevent the onset of disease, by eating well and giving your body the greatest opportunity for good health, you are doing the best you can.

Fresh organic yogurt, containing a live yogurt culture, helps keep your digestion healthy.

A selection of fresh, organic fruit is not only healthy, but looks attractive too.

The suggested breakfast on both retreat schedules is fruit, yogurt and muesli.

Fresh organic fruit is one of the healthiest foods for your body. Choose any fruit that you enjoy eating. If you are keen to detoxify during your home retreat, then melons and grapes aid the body's detoxification process. Raw fruit is ideal, but stewed fruit is also good, especially in winter when it is sensible to eat something hot at each meal. If you dislike the idea of eating fruit early in the day, you have the option of juicing. It is easy to buy an efficient, electric juicing machine, which extracts the goodness of the fruit into the juice and leaves a residue of pulp that can be thrown away. You can create interesting combinations of fruit (and some vegetables) that make delicious, healthy drinks, which give you all the necessary vitamins and health benefits without you having to eat the whole fruit. Try pomegranates and pears, apples and carrots, melons and peaches.

Try to purchase plain, organic live yogurt that contains *Lactobacillus acidophilus*, or a similar yogurt culture, because live yogurt keeps your digestive system healthy. Avoid yogurts that contain fruit and other added ingredients, because they will probably also contain sugar, preservatives, synthetic colourings and flavourings. Sheep and goats' yogurts are preferable, because they are non-mucus-forming. If you don't like their strong taste, then a good organic, live cows' yogurt is fine.

The best muesli is organic and contains a wide range of grains, dried fruit, nuts and seeds. If you can't find a really good organic muesli, you can make up your own mix from scratch, using different base ingredients, or you can buy a fairly basic muesli and add extra ingredients. Nuts and seeds are especially nutritious and contain a lot of trace minerals. Try to include almonds, walnuts, sunflower seeds, sesame seeds, pumpkin seeds and linseeds. If you don't like the crunchy texture of seeds, you can grind them first and then sprinkle the mixture onto your muesli.

◆ basic late-morning schedule

10.00	rest
10.30	re-energizing exercises
11.00	mindfulness meditation
11.30	cup of stimulating herbal tea
11.45	healing meditation using visualization
12.15	rest

✳ classic late-morning schedule

08.30	rest
09.00	skin brushing to stimulate the circulation
09.30	mindfulness meditation
10.00	free dance
10.30	cup of stimulating herbal tea
10.45	healing meditation using visualization
11.15	rest

basic activities are indicated by ◆
classic activities are indicated by ✳

late-morning programme

The first rest period of your home-retreat day signals the start of the late-morning session. There are several rest periods spread throughout the day, and they are important times for relaxation and reflection. However, rest periods are not meant for idleness; or designed for mindless lounging around, for reading, listening to music or other mundane activities – they form an integral part of the retreat activities and do not represent a complete break from the schedule.

meditation and rest

In traditional meditation retreats, rest periods are viewed either as opportunities for informal meditation practice, or as practice outside the formal meditation sessions.

These two descriptions may seem rather confusing at first, and you might think: 'Either you are meditating, or you are not.' However, meditation practice is not as black and white as this 'either/or' attitude would suggest.

During your home retreat you will be practising a variety of different meditation techniques, ranging from the simplicity of calm meditation (see page 52) to the more complex healing meditation using visualization (see page 70). However, these different meditations share common features: they all have a formal structure and methodology. Each meditation requires you to learn a particular technique, and then practise the meditation according to the instructions. There is a clearly defined beginning and end for each session, before you move on to the next retreat activity.

However, meditation is a vast and profound spiritual practice, and not simply a technique or methodology applied at specific times. It is first and foremost a method of transforming the mind and, by so doing, it enables those who practise it to lead happier lives. Yet you cannot spend all your time in formal meditation. Even during a home retreat, when you have spent so much energy on creating the time and space for the purpose of meditating, you still need to prepare food, take a bath, make herbal tea, and so on. This means that there are several periods during your schedule when you are not actually practising one of the formal meditations – and rest periods form one of these.

informal meditation

Perhaps the best way to describe these rest periods is as opportunities to practise informal meditation. In this way you maintain the attention, awareness and spaciousness of your meditation practice when you are not formally meditating. You do not need to sit in the correct posture, or be constantly trying to watch the breath or following other meditation techniques. The rest periods are so called because they give you the chance to relax, but without letting go completely of your meditative frame of mind or connection with your spiritual self.

Meditation is often described as training the mind, so you can regard your informal meditation during rest periods as gentle practice of what you have learned and discovered during your formal sessions. This gives you time to consolidate your experience and work towards understanding how your meditation is progressing. You should of course still rest – and lying down helps the body to recover from the sitting posture and to relax after the movement meditations.

Sitting in a hard back chair for your meditation sessions is a useful alternative to sitting on a cushion on the floor.

letting yourself *be*

During the rest periods your meditation can be as simple as lying down, calmly relaxing both mind and body, but maintaining a gentle awareness of how both are feeling. In this way you remain fully present to what is happening inside you and to your immediate environment. You will notice tiny shifts of mood; the slight change of light when a cloud passes over the sun; and other little details of life that it is so easy to miss when you are just daydreaming or being idle.

Above all, rest periods offer you the precious time and space simply to *be* – even more than the formal meditation sessions do. Daily life does not provide many, if any, opportunities to rest attentively, being fully with yourself as your mind, body and spirit gently shift from one moment to the next. So the rest periods are relaxing and enjoyable, allowing you to rejuvenate while remaining mindful. They give you the chance to discover the happiness of simply being alive in the present moment and to appreciate the world around you.

Rest periods offer you the chance to find happiness by simply appreciating the present moment.

renewing your resolve

By this stage, hopefully, you are feeling pleased to have completed the morning rituals and meditations, and are looking forward to the rest of the home-retreat day. However, you may also be feeling a little tired, restless or lethargic. So this is a good time to spend a few moments renewing your resolve and deepening your commitment to completing the retreat schedule as well as you can.

First of all, reflect on what you have already successfully achieved – which is all of the early-morning activities. Perhaps this gave you your first experience of meditating, or of doing a body scrub, so you have experienced something new. This in itself is a cause for happiness and satisfaction. Even if you were familiar with everything you did this morning, you can still rejoice at the completion of this first part of your home retreat. Feel good about what you have achieved so far.

Now, consider that there are still three more parts of the day to come. Look forward to the opportunity to meditate that you have created for yourself. It is rare to have a whole day devoted to exploring your mind and rejuvenating your body, so feel happy that you still have the remainder of the day to spend on these activities. If you feel any resistance, negativity or even laziness, imagine yourself back in your daily life, completing your usual mundane tasks, and all the normal stresses and tensions of the day. Think how lucky you are to be spending the entire day in a home retreat, away from your regular routine.

Finally, resolve to continue the rest of the day as well as you started it. Generate enthusiastic commitment and joyful determination; feel inspired to meditate for the remainder of the day. Vow to make the most of each sitting meditation and each

Take time to reflect on your retreat experience and appreciate the time you have left to meditate.

physical movement meditation. Appreciate that you will be eating only healthy food and drinking cleansing, refreshing spring water and herbal teas, and that both your mind and body will feel rejuvenated by the end of the day. Reflect that your connection with life will have deepened through your meditation experience, and that you will feel healthy and whole, with body, mind and spirit in complete harmony.

Now it is time to move on to the late-morning rituals and activities.

*skin brushing

It is now time to do some skin brushing, if you are following the classic one-day schedule. Its main purposes are to exfoliate – remove dead skin cells – and stimulate the healthy regeneration of new skin cells.

You can of course include skin brushing in the basic schedule, if you wish to experience its rejuvenating effects and can make time to fit it in. However, you may find that the re-energizing chi kung exercises (see page 66) are sufficiently stimulating at this point of the basic home-retreat schedule.

Skin brushing is rejuvenating for the whole body. Its detoxifying and cleansing effects are the key to good health, increased energy and vitality. Skin brushing also helps your immune system, assisting you in fighting off infection and illness.

Skin brushes are made from natural bristle, and most of them have a long handle so that you can reach down (and up) behind yourself to cover your whole back. Skin brushing is done on dry skin, which creates a different effect from the moistened body scrub you did in the early-morning programme (see page 42). It stimulates the lymphatic system and the circulation of blood, which in turn aids the elimination of impurities from under the surface of the skin. Follow the sequence opposite to cover your entire body.

This skin brush has soft, natural bristles that help to gently remove dead skin cells.

how to use a skin brush

1 To do skin brushing effectively, hold the brush firmly in one hand. Ensure that the entire brush head is in contact with your skin and then make small, brisk, continuous, flowing, rhythmic circles all over your body.

2 Remember that, as part of your home-retreat activities, skin brushing should be done mindfully, with your full attention on what you are doing. Try not to daydream or think of anything other than your current activity. Feel the effects of the skin brushing on your body as you are doing it.

3 Be systematic: start with one leg, then move on to the other, ensuring that you cover the back, sides and front of both legs. Don't forget your feet, knees and ankles, and include your hips and buttocks.

4 Then skin brush both arms and hands, including the elbows, wrists and fingers.

5 Move on to your back, ensuring that you reach right down and up your back to skin brush every part of it; and make sure that you include the back of your neck. (Looking in a mirror can help when skin brushing your back.)

6 Finish with the front of your body, including your abdomen and chest up to your throat. However, avoid your actual throat and face, as the skin there is too delicate for skin brushing.

✦ re-energizing exercises

If you are following the basic schedule, it's now time to do some re-energizing exercises. These simple but powerful exercises are based on traditional chi kung movements, which stimulate different elements in the body.

Chi kung is the Chinese system of movements for promoting the harmonious flow of subtle energies throughout mind, body and spirit. These re-energizing exercises also gently stimulate your energy and stretch your muscles, which may have become cramped from sitting still in meditation. The inner peace you are hopefully experiencing from meditating can turn to lethargy if you are not careful. These movements enable you to continue meditating afterwards with fresh energy and a clear mind, because by this stage of the home retreat your energies may be flagging a little. The exercises are traditionally performed silently and rhythmically, in time with the in-breath and the out-breath.

1 Start by standing with your feet apart, slightly wider than your hips, and your knees softly bent. Check how your shoulders are feeling and make sure they are completely relaxed. Your arms should be hanging loosely at your sides. Exhale fully, emptying your lungs of air.

2 Now, at the start of a long, deep inhalation, slowly and gently bring your hands together and prepare to lift your arms out to the side. Imagine yourself as a male peacock about to extend and display its beautiful coloured feathers. Bend your knees slightly as you begin to breathe.

3 Slowly and mindfully continue to lift your arms to the sides. Make sure you continue to slowly inhale, and that your hands and arms are soft and relaxed. Check that your knees are still softly bent.

4 As you continue the in-breath, bring your arms round to the front of your body. Imagine you are breathing in positive chi energy along with the breath. Then gently and slowly draw your hands in towards your chest.

5 Pause when your palms are close to the front of your body. Turn your palms to face down towards the ground and push them slowly downwards, as you start to breathe out, imagining breathing out negative chi along with the breath.

6 Keep exhaling gently as your hands reach the level of your abdomen. You can imagine you are pushing a float down in water if you start to feel a slight subtle resistance, and in this way work with your subtle energies.

7 As you continue to slowly exhale, try to feel your connection to the ground. At this point you are now ready to start a new sequence. Repeat six to ten times, according to preference. The movements are surprisingly and subtly powerful, and so six sequences may be sufficient the first few times you practise them.

*free dance

Free dancing during a meditation retreat might seem a little unusual, as dancing does not form a part of traditional meditation retreats. However, a home retreat allows you a little more flexibility than a retreat at a meditation centre.

A closer look at the deeper aspects of dancing – beyond modern disco dancing – reveals that it forms an integral part of many tribal and shamanic traditions. During traditional spiritual rituals, dance rhythms and movements (generally accompanied by drumming) are used to facilitate trance-like states, and sometimes to invite spirits to enter the bodies of the dancers. Dance is also used at the end of ceremonies to free people's energies after long periods of focused attention and ritual.

A session of free dance during a spiritual spa helps you connect with, ground and free your subtle and physical energies. Although free dance is unstructured, the movements are done with focused awareness, so your dancing becomes a movement meditation. Meditative music or drumming often facilitates free dance, although you can dance in silence if you prefer.

1 Set your alarm for 30 minutes.

2 Start by standing still and focusing attention on your body, then simply let your body guide you into any dance movements that come to you.

3 Keep your attention on the body; don't think about dancing – simply do it.

A session of free dance during your home retreat helps to release your subtle and physical energies.

✦ ✱ mindfulness meditation

Once the mind has quietened from practising calm meditation, you can deepen the meditation process by being mindful of your feelings and sensations and by being aware of your immediate environment.

1 Start off as you would for practising calm meditation (see page 52), sitting comfortably with a straight back and relaxed in your usual meditation posture. Set your alarm for 30 minutes, close or half-close your eyes, and place your hands in your lap.

2 Now bring your attention to your breathing by becoming aware of the sensation at the tip of your nostrils as you inhale and exhale. Be aware of simply watching the breath, without judging the process in any way. Don't try to change how you breathe; whether your breathing is deep or shallow is unimportant. Just watch your breath for a few minutes.

3 Now let your attention gently expand outwards from your breathing and into your whole body. Be aware of whether you can feel any tension or pain anywhere in the body. Really be *in* your body – check it out and be conscious of all the different sensations, and feelings in the different parts of your body.

4 As you expand your awareness into your body, after a few minutes extend your awareness further and go beyond the body. Be mindful of your immediate environment: how the room feels, the sensation of clothes and air on your skin, and any little sounds that arise and pass. Don't make any judgements; simply note what you feel, and stay with the feelings and sensations for as long as they last.

5 The point of this meditation is to be in the present moment as fully and as authentically as possible. This means being aware of all your physical, emotional and mental processes as they happen, but not being drawn into them. If a sound arises, simply be aware of it, but don't think about it at all. Observe sounds, thoughts and feelings as they arise, and then let them pass.

6 When your mind wanders off into your usual thoughts and sensations, or you become distracted or start to think about your feelings, bring your attention back to your breath for a few minutes then return to practising the mindfulness meditation as described above.

7 When the alarm rings, gently open your eyes and shift your position, taking a few minutes to reflect on your meditation before moving on to the next activity on your schedule.

✦* healing meditation

During your meditations you may experience a wide range of emotions. Although the main purpose of your home retreat is to end up feeling calm, nonetheless meditation is a powerful tool for self-enquiry and spiritual development.

If old, painful memories and unresolved issues occasionally arise in your consciousness, this meditation will help to heal them. Although such feelings may be difficult to process, they do provide an ideal opportunity to heal past pain and trauma. We tend to repress emotions arising from difficult situations, because they often feel too painful to deal with at the time. But the memory lurks on in our unconscious, waiting for an appropriate time to re-enter our conscious mind. The following healing meditation using visualization can help you to accept repressed, painful memories, heal them and then let them go.

soothing essential oils

Burning appropriate essential oils, or aromatic incense, can soothe the painful feelings and facilitate letting them go.

• Frankincense, neroli, rose, cypress, juniper and myrrh are particularly useful for this meditation.

1 Set your alarm for 30 minutes. Start by sitting still in your usual meditation posture and begin by watching the breath. For this meditation bring your attention to the sensations of your abdomen rising and falling with each inhalation and exhalation. Meditate like this for ten minutes.

2 If a painful memory occurred during an earlier meditation session, try to bring it to mind now. Alternatively, consciously recall a difficult situation you would like to heal, such as bereavement or loss of a relationship. Whatever arises in your mind now may benefit from this healing meditation.

3 Allow the painful feelings, or past emotions, to rest in your mind. Reflect that this is something from the past – a recollection of an event – so it has no real power to hurt you now in the present moment. Resolve to heal the pain and let the memory go.

4 Visualize a fountain of infinite pure, white light above your head. The light pours down endlessly over your body and soothes your pain. Visualize the painful emotions emanating from your body as black smoke, which the white light washes away. Practise this visualization for five or ten minutes.

5 Now visualize the fountain of white light streaming upwards, to a heaven or godly realm of your choice. See your inner essence, your soul or spirit, travelling up the stream of white light to your chosen heavenly realm.

6 Once you arrive at your godly realm or heaven, visualize this paradise as the most beautiful, wonderful place you can imagine. See lovely trees and beautiful flowers, deep blue lakes and majestic mountains. Bring to your visualization whatever is beautiful and meaningful from Nature to you. Enjoy this tranquil environment for a few minutes.

7 Now in the distance imagine that you see a magnificent temple, with golden minarets, marble towers or whatever temple or church architecture is spiritually meaningful for you. Taking your time to enjoy your surroundings, walk through the beautiful gardens towards the temple.

8 As you stand on the steps, pause awhile. Resolve that when you enter the temple you will leave all your painful feelings behind. Mentally apologize to anyone (including yourself) who was hurt by any difficult situation, and try to let all trauma from this situation vanish for ever.

9 Inside the temple is an altar. On the altar is a sacred chalice filled with divine, healing nectar. Imagine drinking the nectar, and feel its healing power radiating through your mind, body and spirit. Feel at peace with yourself: calm, whole and able to fully engage with life again.

10 Now leave the temple and slowly walk towards the fountain of light. Visualize yourself travelling down the stream of white light, then see yourself sitting in meditation, with an aura of white light surrounding you. Feel that you have fully participated in this healing ceremony and have let go of your repressed, painful emotions. Imagine that you have received a divine, spiritual blessing and can now move on with your life in peace.

11 Finish by watching the breath, observing the sensations of your abdomen rising and falling, for five minutes. When the alarm rings, take your time before getting up and moving on to the next home-retreat activity.

Visualize a beautiful scene from Nature similar to this one, during the healing meditation.

late-morning rituals

The late-morning session gives you ample opportunity to make some offerings on your altar, refocus your attention and energy on your sacred space, and use different essential oils for the various sitting and movement meditations.

At an appropriate time during your late-morning session, when a natural break occurs between meditations, spend a few minutes focusing your attention on how your sacred space is feeling. A room that is used regularly for meditation has a serene, spiritual atmosphere – especially when a sacred space and altar have been created within it. However, meditation sometimes facilitates painful or negative emotions to arise, which can affect the atmosphere of a room.

If you feel that the room's atmosphere has lost some of the pure, rarefied feeling that you created with your earlier rituals, you can perform a simple purifying rite. First, open the window for a few minutes to let in some fresh air and to blow away any stale air. This will freshen the tainted atmosphere. Then, after closing the window, slowly and mindfully walk round the boundaries of your sacred space, holding a lighted candle carefully in front of you. You can also burn juniper essential oil in your oil burner, or some purifying incense sticks or cones on your altar.

You may well be making offerings of vaporized essential oils, or incense smoke, and renewing the water bowl on your altar with fresh water, before each meditation session. Alternatively, you may have chosen to have a very simple altar, and only to

You can make up a blend of essential oils in a perfume base to wear during your meditation sessions.

make offerings at the beginning of each day. Whatever you have decided to do, spend a few minutes at some point during the late morning making sure that your altar is clean of incense dust, drops of essential oil, flower petals, and so on. This simple cleaning ritual offers respect to your higher spiritual aspirations and, as you perform it, you can reaffirm your intention to make the most of your meditation during this home retreat.

using essential oils during meditation

In the instructions given for using essential oils (see page 35) it was recommended that you vaporize the oils in a burner. However, there are other ritual ways of using essential oils that can be equally appropriate for some of the different sitting and movement meditations. So, before you begin each session (whether a sitting or movement meditation), you need to decide which method is most appropriate in that specific instance.

The main ways of using essential oils are in a burner, in a room spray or in a blend that you apply to your body:

- A burner is in many instances the most effective method, because the diffused essential oils give off a powerful aroma.

- A room spray is the most appropriate choice if you want to create a very subtle effect.

- Surrounding yourself with the fragrance of your own special blend of essential oils, by wearing them like a perfume, is a really useful method when you practise the walking meditation

An essential oil burner is the most effective method of diffusing the essential oils.

(see page 96) or any of the other movement meditations.

essential oil burners

How to prepare your essential oil burner before meditating has already been described (see page 35), and you should follow those instructions before each meditation session during which you will vaporize essential oils by this method. Then you

essential oils for fatigue

- If you are feeling tired, dull, lazy or lethargic, the most important purpose of essential oils is to stimulate and refresh your senses during the meditation so that you do not fall asleep.

- In this instance you would choose a mentally stimulating essential oil such as rosemary, cardamom, black pepper or basil, and blend it with an uplifting and refreshing essential oil, such as bergamot, orange or grapefruit; you would also include a harmonizing and balancing essential oil, such as geranium or rosewood.

Room sprays with essential oils combined in water give you a very subtle effect.

need to decide which essential oils, or combination of oils, you are going to use. Remember that all these preparations are an integral part of the home retreat, and should be done in a reflective, meditative and ritualistic manner.

First, analyse how you are feeling before you start your meditation session, and reflect on the nature of this particular meditation technique. After reflecting on what you wish to gain by using essential oils, choose three or four oils according to your feelings. Smell each essential oil carefully to make sure the fragrance is pleasing to you and feels appropriate for the meditation. Float your chosen essential oils on top of the water, as described. Using cold water allows you to begin your meditation as the water slowly heats, so the

essential oils diffuse gradually. However, if you prefer a more instant effect, you can use hot water so that the essential oils vaporize quickly. Once you have set your alarm and are ready to begin your meditation session, light the candle.

room sprays

If you don't particularly like the aroma of essential oils, or you prefer a very faint fragrance, you should use a room spray. You can achieve a much more subtle effect with this method. Choose your essential oils carefully, as described opposite, then add up to 60 drops per 100 ml (3½ fl oz) of water in your spray bottle, and shake well (see page 35). Once you have set your alarm and are ready to start meditating, spray the room with the mixture of essential oils and water.

perfume blends

When you are doing any of the movement meditations, such as the re-energizing chi kung exercises (see page 66) or the free dance (see page 68) during the late-morning session, wearing a blend of essential oils is very effective. This method surrounds you with the gentle fragrance of your chosen blend, wherever you are in the room.

Take a small, dark glass bottle of approximately 10 ml (2 teaspoons) – such as an empty essential oil bottle – and almost fill it with almond oil. Then carefully choose whichever essential oils you wish to use, and add up to 15 drops to the bottle. Mix the essential oils thoroughly into the almond oil by shaking the bottle. Then use your fingertips to apply the blend behind your ears, to the base of your throat and the inside of your wrists.

essential oils for perfume blends

- For the chi kung exercise, you might choose from frankincense, sandalwood, vetiver, myrrh, lavender and jasmine.

- For the free-dance exercise, you might select some of the following: geranium, lemon, lavender, sandalwood and petitgrain.

Try dabbing perfume made with essential oils behind your ears and on the inside of your wrists.

herbal teas

You will probably feel quite thirsty after doing the various movement meditations of the late-morning session, especially the free-dance exercise, which can end up being surprisingly energetic.

You should of course relieve your thirst at suitable points throughout the day, even if a drink is not specifically listed at that time. However, do not interrupt the flow of any of the sitting or movement meditations – wait until the end of a particular meditation or exercise before stopping to take a suitable hot or cold drink.

Before you start your home retreat, you should purchase several large bottles of pure spring or mineral water. Still bottled water is best, although if you particularly like sparkling mineral water, that is also fine. This natural water should be drunk whenever you feel thirsty. It is a good idea to drink a lot of spring water during your home retreat because this will help your body purify itself and flush out toxins; it also helps your complexion to become clear and your eyes to look bright, as well as cleansing the different body systems and organs.

If you are undertaking your home retreat in the summer and the weather is warm, you do not need to have a hot drink during the late-morning session – you can just drink a glass of bottled water. However, in the winter it is a good idea to take a hot drink. This might be simply hot water, or hot water with freshly squeezed lemon juice – the same drink you took in the early morning (see page 55).

ginger infusions

A pleasant alternative to herbal tea is an infusion of ginger, which makes a refreshing, stimulating and warming drink.

Ginger has various health benefits that you may find of use during your home retreat. For instance, if you are feeling cold from sitting still in meditation, an infusion of ginger is generally warming and stimulates the circulation. It also promotes good digestion, relieves nausea and mild digestive upsets. If you feel you have a cold coming on, regular hot infusions of ginger may help to prevent its onset and relieve coughing.

Grating fresh root ginger is an alternative to thinly slicing it for making an infusion.

how to make an infusion

1 Take a piece of fresh (preferably organic) root ginger about the size of your thumb. Scrape off the thin layer of peel, then slice the root ginger thinly.

2 Put the slices into a china teapot and pour over sufficient boiling water to fill a mug.

3 Leave the mixture to steep for five minutes, then strain it into a mug. You can add a teaspoon or two of honey to taste, if you like, or a squeeze of fresh lemon juice (or both, according to preference).

late morning herbal teas

- If you enjoy drinking herbal teas, there is a wide range to choose from, or you can be creative and invent your own mixture from a selection of loose, dried herbs. To help you decide which herbal tea or combination you would like to drink, assess how you are feeling at this stage of the day.

- If you are feeling lively and energized from the movement exercises, you might want to choose a calming blend. An especially soothing, balancing blend – but one that will not make you feel too soporific – is a mixture of camomile and peppermint. There are several proprietary brands of this blend, or you can make your own.

- If you are feeling a little jaded, try a mixture of rosehip and hibiscus. Proprietary brands of this refreshing blend are also available.

A soothing, balancing cup of camomile and peppermint herbal tea is a suitable drink for the late morning.

✦ basic afternoon schedule

12.30	prepare vegetables and tofu (or soak beans) and brown rice for lunch
13.00	cook and eat lunch
14.00	rest
14.30	brisk, vigorous walk
15.15	calm meditation (see page 52)
15.45	cup of herbal tea
16.00	write about your feelings and experiences, in creative free writing or journaling exercise
16.30	insight meditation
17.00	rest

✱ classic afternoon schedule

11.30	prepare vegetables and tofu (or soak beans) and brown rice for lunch
12.00	cook and eat lunch
13.00	rest
13.30	brisk, vigorous walk
14.15	calm meditation (see page 52)
14.45	walking meditation
15.15	cup of herbal tea
15.30	re-energizing exercises
16.00	write about your feelings and experiences, in creative free writing or journaling exercise
16.30	insight meditation
17.00	relaxing exercises

basic activities are indicated by ✦
classic activities are indicated by ✱

afternoon programme

The start of the afternoon session marks the psychological mid-point of your home-retreat day. You have now completed approximately half of the meditations and exercises, and therefore still have half a day in which to complete the remaining practices. You are probably feeling quite hungry at this stage, and thoughts of preparing and eating a meal are likely to arise frequently. So this is a good time for reflection: first, on the halfway stage of your spiritual spa; and second, on the purpose of taking nourishment by eating your main meal at this stage of the day.

maintaining your motivation

The rest period during the afteroon session provides a useful opportunity for reflection and rumination while you relax and read your retreat contract.

It is a good idea during this rest period to check your motivation levels and assess how you are feeling. Successfully completing a home-retreat day requires a substantial amount of self-discipline. At meditation centres your motivation to complete the whole retreat is stimulated by the presence of other retreatants, and by the inspiration and guidance of your meditation teachers.

During a home retreat you have neither the silent, companionable support of fellow retreatants, nor the leadership and guidance of a teacher to keep your motivational levels up. This means that you alone have to generate all the necessary enthusiasm to successfully complete the retreat. Maintaining your commitment throughout the day can be difficult – this is why you drew up and signed a contract with yourself to complete the retreat day. If you find your energy or motivation flagging at this halfway stage, get out your contract and read through it. This will remind you of all the reasons why you decided to undertake a home retreat in the first place, and will help you banish any thoughts of abandoning it before it is finished.

As you read through your contract, you may find that you have discovered new reasons for wanting to meditate. You may also notice that one of your original reasons is not quite as valid or as relevant as you first thought. There is nothing wrong with either of these changes; coming up with new reasons for

wishing to meditate, or modifying your original intentions, is simply part of the ongoing process of the mind – and this is especially noticeable during a retreat, when you are observing the mind during your meditations. It is part of the mind's nature to change constantly: all thoughts and feelings are impermanent. However, if your original motivation for meditating remains sincere, then your fundamental reasons for wishing to meditate will still ring true.

going with the flow

Later on in the day there is a reflective writing or journaling exercise, and you may wish to note down some of your feelings, doubts and inspirations during that session. At this point try to resist any desire to write changes into your contract, or to jot down any new ideas and reasons for wishing to meditate. Stay with the silent reflection and contemplation, and simply watch the mind and the ever-changing flow of thoughts and feelings as you rest. If you still feel a little lethargic, resistant or lazy after reading through your contract, then mentally renew your commitment to continue with the meditations and exercises until the day's schedule is completed.

On the other hand, you may not feel the need to read through your contract to remind yourself why you are undertaking a home retreat. Your sitting and

Reading through your contract reminds you of your
reasons for wanting to undertake a home retreat.

movement meditations may have gone well up to this point, and you may be feeling tranquil, energized, inspired and positive. In this situation, simply enjoy your rest period and gently observe the mind, your feelings and your body, noticing all the subtle changes as they occur.

There is no point in judging your experience as 'good' or 'bad'. Even experienced meditators have off-days when their meditation does not flow, when negative mind states and feelings arise and it is difficult to remain motivated. Conversely, someone relatively new to meditation can have a really positive experience and find the various meditations pleasant and flowing well. The point of meditation is simply to stay with whatever thoughts and feelings arise, without judging or trying to change your experience in any way. This calm attention to what is – rather than what you might like it to be – has many long-term benefits, and is one major reason to keep meditating regularly and frequently.

taking time for lunch and rest

In the period shortly before preparing food and eating your meal, the main thoughts and feelings that are likely to arise in your mind and body concern hunger, and the desire to relieve this sensation by eating.

Hunger may make it difficult to concentrate on your meditation, because all you want to do is eat. However, these feelings provide a good opportunity to enquire into the body's requirements for food. Normally, if you feel hunger, your first instinct is to relieve it by eating as soon as you can and as much as you wish. However, when you are undertaking a home retreat take some time to consider the deeper meanings and issues concerning food.

As mentioned earlier, it is important to eat well during a home-retreat day. However, this does not mean eating too much food, or snacking whenever you feel like it. It is also important to eat the right types of food, and avoid the wrong types of food, during a home retreat. This means eating foods that provide adequate nourishment that the body slowly assimilates, providing energy over a long period of time. You also need to avoid any foods that contain high levels of sugar, as the body may develop a 'sugar rush'. After this has passed, you will feel the need to eat more, when in fact your body simply needs to readjust to its normal metabolic rate. It's a good idea to avoid refined carbohydrates and high levels of salt and fats, and eat mostly natural wholegrains, fresh fruit and vegetables.

You will eat only a small amount in the early evening and will have your main meal in the middle of the day, which may be quite different from your usual eating patterns. Taking these facts into consideration means that during a home-retreat day you adopt a neutral approach to eating: neither starving yourself in the misguided view that this will improve your meditation, nor eating too much food or too heavily in the evening. In this way your body receives sufficient nourishment to function well, but does not become overly full, or bloated and soporific in the evening.

The afternoon session allows sufficient time to prepare and cook fresh, nourishing food; time to eat the meal slowly and with mindful awareness; then a rest period in which your body can properly digest the food. In this way both mind and body receive adequate nourishment in the middle of the day, as well as a complete break from mediation and all the other spiritual spa activities of your schedule. Once lunchtime is over, you will feel refreshed and ready to complete your home-retreat day.

Eating a healthy meal in the middle of the day maintains your energy levels for the rest of the day's meditations.

food and drink

Eating your main meal in the middle of the day, and taking sufficient time to rest and digest immediately afterwards, is beneficial not only to your body, but also to your meditation.

In everyday life people tend to eat a small lunch quickly and then carry straight on with the rest of their day's work. Then they eat a big meal in the evening, when their minds and bodies are tired. Eating a large quantity of food when you are tired causes sluggishness, and many people tend to spend a drowsy evening watching television, reading or engaged in other passive pastimes. Eating a light meal in the evening means that both mind and body stay more alert and it is easier to maintain high levels of concentration in your later meditation sessions.

foods to nourish mind and body

Modern culture has brought us pre-packaged convenience food, and instant-gratification fast food, both of which are usually full of saturated fats, salt and sugar. Most damagingly, these foods also contain a cocktail of chemical additives, many of which can be toxic for the body.

However, when you consider that the whole food chain is contaminated by the addition of chemical additives at each stage of production, the scenario gets much worse. Plant seeds are

Beans and pulses contain protein, and therefore make a good substitute for eating meat or fish.

These fresh, organic parsnips will taste great as part of either of the two main meal recipes suggested.

routinely coated with chemicals to promote rapid growth and repel insects, then crops are sprayed with various pesticides. When we eat these crops, we also eat the chemicals – many of which remain in the cells of our bodies. Furthermore, the animals that eat these crops ingest the chemical additives, a number of which are stored in their body tissues; so if you eat their meat, you are absorbing two levels of additives. Animals are also regularly injected with antibiotics and growth hormones, and their meat frequently contains preservatives and colourants.

What can you do to improve your diet? The first place to start is by eating foods that are as close as possible to their natural state; these will contain naturally occurring vitamins and minerals, and there is less chance of them being contaminated with pesticides and other chemical additives. This means eating lots of fresh fruit and vegetables (some of which should regularly be eaten raw). Most importantly, buying and eating organic foodstuffs whenever possible eliminates the dangers of chemical additives. Wholegrain foods, such as brown rice and wholemeal bread, are good for you because they are high in natural fibre and therefore help to prevent constipation. Drinking lots of fresh spring water and herbal teas, and reducing your intake of caffeine drinks, are also of great benefit to the body.

vegetarian benefits

Most Western adults eat more protein than they actually need in order to stay healthy, and most of this comprises meat and fish. Reducing or eliminating meat from your diet lessens your

Drinking lots of fresh spring or mineral water is of great benefit to the body.

protein intake. Eating less red meat also reduces your intake of animal fats, which various scientific studies have proven to contribute to high blood pressure and coronary disease. There are many healthy alternative proteins available, such as nuts, soya products and pulses; and free-range, organic fish and chicken are less toxic and more healthy than red meat.

There are other unhealthy foods that you need to eliminate from your diet, or cut down on. These include refined flour (found in white bread, cakes and biscuits), sugar, salt, caffeine, and those chemical additives listed as E-numbers on pre-packaged foods. Most of us could benefit from eating less fat, and the fats that we do eat should be unsaturated and of vegetable origin, such as extra-virgin olive oil for cooking and dressing salads, and organic sunflower spread instead of butter. Of course, such a healthy diet is difficult to stick to at all times, but it does serve as a good basis for nutritious eating.

Giving up meat and pre-packaged foods laced with salt, sugar and artificial flavours can lead to bland-tasting meals, but the addition of herbs and other natural flavourings (such as ground sesame

Whole grains, like this long grain brown rice, are good for maintaining a healthy digestion.

seeds) can help. Not only are herbs good for you, but they add natural flavour to many dishes. Most culinary herbs stimulate and aid the digestion and have been used in cooking for many generations.

meal-planning suggestions

A good main meal to eat during your retreat is listed in both home-retreat schedules, and consists of tofu or beans with vegetables and brown rice. However, an alternative recipe is also given to cater for different tastes and to offer you some variety. You can of course devise your own main meal, although recipes should be based on the suggested foods. A side salad can be added if you wish. Before starting your spiritual spa, read through the two different meal options and decide which one you prefer – or choose both, if you are undertaking a longer retreat. You then need to buy in the various ingredients for all the meals before you actually start your retreat.

You will notice that the suggested meals are both vegetarian. Not only is this a healthy choice, but a home retreat has a pronounced spiritual aspect – and spirituality involves ethics. Although not all religions proscribe eating meat for ethical reasons, most meditation centres offer only vegetarian (or even vegan) meals. This means that during your retreat you are not involved with, or implicated in, the killing of any animals to provide you with food. Even if you normally choose to eat meat, during your retreat you can follow the principle of doing no harm to other living beings.

In India and many other Asian countries, religious practice is traditionally integrated into daily life to a great extent. Much of the population is vegetarian, due to a combination of religious

Remember to have a focused, mindful awareness when you are chopping vegetables, similar to meditation.

principles, cultural tradition and poverty. Some of the ancient religious texts also suggest that eating meat is not conducive to meditation, and this principle has been incorporated into many meditation retreats in the West. These texts also favour not eating overly stimulating or 'black' foods such as garlic, so this is also omitted from the recipes given overleaf.

tofu or beans with vegetables and brown rice

ingredients (all preferably organic)

½ packet tofu or 75 g (3 oz) aduki, kidney, borlotti
    or other beans

a little sunflower, olive or other vegetable oil

200 g (7 oz) short- or long-grain brown rice

1 large carrot, turnip or other root vegetable,
    scraped and chopped

6 florets broccoli or cauliflower

1 small onion, finely chopped

1 red or yellow pepper, chopped

1 courgette, chopped

6 mushrooms, chopped

2 tomatoes, chopped

handful of fresh mixed herbs, finely chopped

1 tablespoon tahini

*Tofu, also commonly called bean curd, is a low fat,
healthy source of vegetable protein.*

method

1 Drain the packet of tofu, then halve the block and store the spare half in a bowl of water in the refrigerator. Cut the remaining tofu into small cubes, and fry in half of the oil for a few minutes on each side. Drain and place to one side. Alternatively, if you are using beans, soak them in a bowl with sufficient water to cover them the night before your home-retreat day starts. The next day wash the beans and boil in fresh water for 30 minutes, or until soft.

2 Wash the brown rice thoroughly. Place it in a saucepan with sufficient water to cover it, then bring to the boil and allow to simmer for 20–30 minutes.

3 Place the carrot or other root vegetable, and the broccoli or cauliflower, in a steamer above the rice. Remove when soft and put to one side with the tofu.

4 Fry the onion in the remaining oil for a few minutes, then add the pepper and courgette. Fry for a few minutes more, then add the mushrooms, tomatoes and herbs. You may need to add a little water if the mixture is too dry.

5 Once all these vegetables are cooked, add the root vegetable, broccoli or cauliflower, tahini and tofu or beans, and mix well.

6 Cover and leave for a few minutes, then serve the mixture on top of the rice. If you require more flavour, add a little soy sauce, ground pepper or ground sesame seed.

spicy vegetables with couscous

ingredients (all preferably organic)

1 small leek, finely chopped

1 carrot, cut into chunks

1 parsnip, cut into chunks

1 courgette, cut into chunks

1 red or yellow pepper, cut into chunks

handful of finely chopped, fresh mixed herbs

½ can chickpeas

100 g (4 oz) shredded cabbage or other greens

200 g (7 oz) couscous

1 teaspoon harissa paste

method

1 Put all the vegetables, except the cabbage, in a casserole with the herbs and with sufficient water to cover them. Add the lid and place the casserole in a preheated oven, 200°C (400°F), Gas Mark 6, for 40 minutes.

2 Remove the casserole from the oven and check that the vegetables are soft, then add the chickpeas to the mixture and return to the oven for 5 minutes.

3 Cook the cabbage or other greens in a steamer for 5 minutes.

4 Place the couscous in a bowl, pour over sufficient boiling water to cover it, then place a folded tea towel on top to steam it. Leave for 5 minutes.

Serve couscous with spicy vegetables for a healthy and satisfying afternoon meal.

5 To serve, fluff the couscous with a fork and arrange on a plate. Remove the casserole from the oven and stir in the harissa paste. Spoon the spicy vegetables over the couscous and serve the cabbage alongside. If you require more flavour, add a little soy sauce, ground black pepper or ground sesame seed.

eating ritual

Eating the main meal during a retreat is often secretly regarded as the highlight of the day. It is appropriate to enjoy your food, but during a meditation retreat eating is done in a thoughtful, ritual fashion with awareness.

1 Once you have served the meal, pause before starting to eat, although this may run against your natural instincts of wanting to eat immediately. Take time to offer thanks to the environment and to all the people involved in growing and producing the food.

2 Reflect on the bountiful gifts of Nature, how the vegetables and grains you are about to eat required fertile soil, sun and rain in order to grow and ripen.

3 Silently offer your gratitude to everything and everyone involved in making it possible for you to sit and eat this meal and generate good wishes for the welfare of the environment and all people.

4 Now reflect on how many people living in the world do not have sufficient food to eat. Think how lucky and privileged you are to have the luxury of eating this healthy, nutritious meal. Generate compassion for those people who have no means of satisfying their hunger, and generate the wish that they may soon find enough food to eat.

5 Now eat your meal, slowly and mindfully. Feel the taste of the food in your mouth, chew each mouthful thoroughly and be aware of the sensations as you swallow your food and it begins its journey around your digestive system.

6 At the end of your meal, again offer gratitude for being able to eat and satisfy your hunger. If you could not finish the meal, save and store what remains. Try not to be unduly wasteful of the precious resource of food.

Eating a meal slowly and mindfully is a ritual of thoughtful activity.

resting and digesting

Now that you have completed your meal, it's time to rest and digest. We don't usually think about our digestion, unless we are ill. However, giving yourself sufficient time to properly digest a meal is of great benefit to your body.

Unfortunately, it is common to see people eating as they walk about, which can cause indigestion and heartburn, because the body does not have enough rest to properly digest the food, and over time such bad habits can lead to digestive malfunctions. During your home retreat time is allotted to rest and digest properly.

1 Once you have mindfully cleared up from your meal, sit down in a firm but comfortable chair. Adopt a posture in which you are leaning back slightly, to allow your digestive system adequate space to process the food. Avoid leaning forward at all, because this cramps the digestive system.

2 Bring your attention to your body and the sensations within it. Feel the digestive process as it unfolds: the stomach gurgling; the intestines expanding gently with the food; the sated feeling from alleviating your hunger. Many people find it calming to rest their hands on their belly during this digestive process, so try this if you like.

3 Towards the end of your rest period, gently rub your belly in a clockwise direction – the same direction in which the food is digested. This action can feel comforting, and gently stimulates your digestion.

4 At the end of the rest period, stand up and walk around to awaken mind and body, and to prepare yourself for moving on to the next session.

Sitting comfortably in a supportive chair after your meal helps to aid digestion.

✦* journaling exercise

This exercise gives you time and space to write about old, repressed or current problematic issues and emotions that may have surfaced in your mind during your late morning meditation sessions.

Writing about these issues is also a preparation for the insight meditation session later on (see page 97). If nothing notable has arisen for you, try doing the creative free-writing exercise (see opposite), instead.

1 Start by noting down in a few words (and in separate sections) any feelings, sensations, new ideas, doubts or other concerns that you have in your mind.

2 Read through each phrase slowly until one in particular strikes you as being the most interesting or important, and the one you wish to explore further.

3 Focus on this phrase, and start to jot down any feelings or questions about it. Don't worry about writing proper sentences, or about the grammar; simply note down words, phrases and images as they arise in your mind.

4 Once you reach a natural pause, stop writing. Spend a few minutes simply watching the breath in calm meditation (see page 52) until you feel soothed and grounded.

5 Read through slowly what you have written. It doesn't need to be logical or make complete sense, as long as it is meaningful to you.

6 Now edit and rewrite what you have written into a clear, structured paragraph. This will further clarify your feelings about the idea or issue, which you can then explore in greater depth during insight meditation.

Take the opportunity to jot down any feelings or concerns and then focus on one issue that arises.

✦✱ creative free writing

If no problematic emotions or issues have surfaced, then creative ideas and thoughts may have arisen instead. This free-writing exercise offers you time to write down any such ideas so that you can develop them later, if you wish.

1 Take a blank sheet of paper and a pen. Set your alarm for five minutes, then start writing down any words, images, thoughts, sensations or ideas that come to mind. Don't worry about structure, grammar or mistakes; the important thing is not to stop writing.

2 If you go blank, keep writing down the last word until a new word or phrase springs to mind. Write down anything at all, remembering not to stop until the alarm rings.

3 Once the bell rings, stop. Read through what you have written and select the concept or phrase that seems most interesting or meaningful.

4 Write down on a new sheet of paper the concept or phrase you have chosen, then develop it by writing creatively and freely about it until you half-fill (or even fill) the page.

5 Read through your writing mindfully. If you wish, you can reflect upon the subject during your insight meditation.

Creative free writing allows you to express your thoughts and ideas as they arise in your mind.

✦* take a walk

Eating, resting and digesting can make you feel quite lazy, and negative thoughts of abandoning your home retreat may arise. The temptation to give into such feelings can, however, easily be counteracted by taking a brisk walk.

After proper time to rest and digest following your lunch, a period of stimulating exercise helps to restore enthusiasm and refresh your motivation to complete the home retreat.

Maintaining your inner boundaries may prove challenging on your walk, as you will need to leave your sacred space and go outside. If you live somewhere rural, you may know a good route where you are unlikely to encounter other people. You should, of course, choose the quietest local walk possible. For those who live in towns, encountering others will be unavoidable. In this instance you need to focus solely on the activity of walking, and not look up at other people whom you see along the way.

As with all the home-retreat activities, taking a vigorous walk should be done with mindful awareness. Make sure you know your route, and walk only for the allotted time.

1 Start off walking at a brisk but sustainable pace. Keep your eyes lowered if you become aware of other people close by, otherwise enjoy looking at the views you encounter.

2 As you walk, be aware of your surroundings: notice the details of the path, the trees or buildings you pass, what the weather is like. You may notice that your usual familiar walk appears a little different because you are seeing it with a more meditative frame of mind. However, don't get distracted by what you see, and be conscious of your walking and of when you need to start returning home.

3 Once you have completed your walk, you should feel invigorated and refreshed. Drink a glass or two of spring water before moving on to the next activity.

A beautiful wood is the perfect place for a meditative walk, if you are lucky enough to live near one.

*walking meditation

Walking meditation is often alternated with sitting meditation and is regarded as an alternative posture, rather than a different activity. If you have a bad back, walking meditation allows you to do as much meditation as you like.

Walking meditation isn't about going anywhere – the point is simply the walking. It is traditionally done in a short straight line, with a pause at the end when you turn round and walk back.

1 Choose a walking path of 5 m (16 ft) or walk in a circle, and use the starting point to change direction. Set your alarm for 30 minutes then stand at the beginning of the line and spend a couple of minutes watching your breath. Slowly and mindfully lift one foot and move it forward, feeling all the muscles that are involved, then place it down, feeling the heel and toes separately as they contact the ground.

If sitting meditation is becoming uncomfortable, try walking meditation instead.

2 Repeat this slow stepping forward until you reach the end of your line – or the point where you began your circle. Then pause, turn, pause and retrace your steps. Keep your arms hanging loosely at your sides or folded lightly over your belly, and your eyes focused down a few steps ahead of you.

3 As you walk, be aware of all the sensations in your body: feel your muscles moving and the sensation of the ground beneath your feet. Be completely present to the whole experience.

4 When the alarm rings, continue walking until you reach the end of the line. Then stand and spend a few minutes watching your breath before moving on to the next home-retreat session.

✦* insight meditation

Practising calm meditation, then gradually deepening the practice with mindfulness meditation will bring some inner tranquillity. You can deepen the process further with insight meditation, and observe the mind more clearly.

Insight meditation involves looking closely at your thoughts and feelings, analysing them and making a mental note of any habitual patterns. We usually identify with our thoughts unquestioningly. Practising insight meditation helps you to see your often habitual thought patterns as merely transient contents of the mind.

Insight meditation goes deeper than calm meditation, helping you to explore your mind.

1 Sit comfortably in your usual meditation posture, set your alarm for 30 minutes, then watch your breath for a few minutes.

2 Gradually become aware of your thoughts and feelings as they arise and pass. Notice how they are fleeting and insubstantial. Now bring your attention to whatever arises in your mind. Concentrate on the image, trying to go beyond your normal superficial attention. Try to analyse the thought or feeling; investigate it thoroughly to gain some insight into it.

3 If you become distracted, return to watching the breath for a few minutes. When you practise insight meditation, repressed memories may surface in your mind, which can be painful. If this happens, remind yourself the painful memory is as insubstantial as any other thought. Simply let it go, and if you feel upset, watch the breath for a few minutes before resuming insight meditation.

4 When your alarm rings, spend a few minutes watching the breath. Open your eyes gently, reflect upon your experience and take your time getting up and moving on.

*relaxing exercise

The following simple exercise, called 'child pose', helps to release tension and promote deep relaxation. This asana is particularly effective after sitting for a long time in meditation, as the curling posture releases any tension in the spine. To do the asana you need to be on your yoga mat, if you have one, or on the carpet or a folded blanket or quilt.

1 Set the alarm for the usual 30 minutes. Start by kneeling on all fours with your knees and hands about the same width as your body. Your head should be in a straight line with the rest of your spine. Ensure all your fingers are spread evenly on the mat, as this will help share the weight of your torso with the heels of your hands and your wrists. The tops of your feet should be relaxed on the mat. Now draw in your stomach and abdominal region towards your spine.

2 Take a deep inhalation to relax and prepare yourself for the next part of the asana. Then exhale as you ease slowly backwards until your buttocks are resting on your heels. At the same time lean forwards until your head touches the mat, and stretch your arms out along the ground in front of you. You should feel a comfortable stretch along your lower spine. Relax your shoulders and ensure your belly remains hollowed in order to support the spine.

3 Now move one arm behind you, relaxing the back of your hand on to the mat. The palm should face upwards at first, then gently allow the fingers to relax into a natural cupping around the sole of the foot on the same side. Your shoulder should now be fully relaxed.

4 Now move the other arm behind you, then relax and cup the foot in the same way. Hold the pose for between three and five breaths, or for however long is comfortable for you. You can use your breathing to help your body sink further into the pose, which will further release tension from your spine, thighs, hips and calves. The deeper you breathe in and out, the lower you will sink in the pose.

5 To finish off this exercise in a really relaxed way, lie still with your head supported on a small pillow, with legs slightly apart and arms slightly away from your body. Watch the breath in calm meditation until the alarm rings. Then get up slowly, do a few stretches to ease your muscles, or walk around a little to ready yourself for the next home-retreat session.

✦ basic evening schedule

17.30	prepare vegetables and make soup, dry-roast a handful of nuts and seeds, then mix with a handful of dried fruit
18.00	mindfulness meditation
18.30	eat supper with a cup of herbal tea
19.00	rest
19.15	walking meditation
19.45	loving-kindness meditation
20.15	relaxing exercises
20.45	bath with essential oils
21.15	meditation on watching the light fade (may be moved earlier in the evening, depending on your location and the time of year)
21.45	chanting, mantra meditation or prayers
22.15	bedtime, with a cup of calming herbal tea

✳ classic evening schedule

17.30	prepare vegetables and make soup, dry-roast a handful of nuts and seeds, then mix with a handful of dried fruit
18.00	calm meditation
18.30	eat supper with a cup of herbal tea
19.00	simple yoga stretching exercises
19.30	mindfulness meditation
20.00	relaxing exercises
20.30	loving-kindness meditation
21.00	bath with essential oils
21.30	meditation on watching the light fade (may be moved earlier in the evening, depending on your location and the time of year)
22.00	chanting, mantra meditation or prayers
22.30	bedtime, with a cup of calming herbal tea

basic activities are indicated by ✦
classic activities are indicated by ✳

evening programme

The evening session takes you from late afternoon right up to bedtime, so it is the last one of your home-retreat day. By this stage you will already have completed quite a lot of the meditations, rituals and exercises of your spiritual spa. There are, however, still various practices to complete before you go to bed. These include preparing and eating a light meal, taking a relaxing bath with essential oils and undertaking some new meditation techniques, as well as repeating some of the meditations with which you are by now familiar.

reflection on a positive achievement

At this point of the day you are likely to be feeling deeply relaxed and tranquil. Although you have not quite finished your home-retreat day, nonetheless you have completed the greater part of it, so you may well be feeling a sense of satisfaction that you have actually reached this point.

With a little extra motivation and energy you can finish the remaining meditations and go to bed knowing that you have successfully accomplished your entire day's schedule.

If this is your first-ever experience of any kind of meditation retreat and you have diligently been following the schedule, you are to be congratulated on your achievement. It might not sound like a great deal when you first read through the home-retreat schedules, but actually getting through either of the day schedules properly – without cheating at all – requires a real sense of commitment and dedication to your spiritual spa.

Even if you already have some previous experience of doing a retreat at a meditation centre, successfully completing your first retreat day at home is something you can feel a positive sense of achievement about. Undertaking a spiritual spa at home means that you must spend a lot of time and energy preparing everything beforehand, creating your sacred space, then looking after yourself by cooking and so on during the day. You must also motivate yourself to undertake all the sessions properly, without the support of other retreatants or a meditation teacher.

If you have done a home retreat before, you were probably well prepared for this retreat and knew what to expect, how to keep your motivation going and how to pace yourself throughout the day. Nonetheless, each such event is a unique experience, bringing with it new challenges and difficulties, as well as fresh high points and feelings of euphoria. If this is merely the latest of several home retreats that you have done, you should still – hopefully – be feeling a sense of satisfaction and achievement.

At this stage of your home retreat day you are likely to feel a real sense of accomplishment.

food and drink

A light, healthy evening meal or snack should be sufficient during the evening session as you will have eaten a substantial main meal at lunchtime.

The evening meal is more of a light snack than a heavy repast. Because you have already eaten your main meal at lunchtime, it is unlikely you will be feeling very hungry at this stage of the day. The foods you ate at lunch were healthy, substantial and nourishing and provided sufficient sustenance for the whole day.

The evening snack

You can reflect that many monastics – especially those following the Theravada tradition of Buddhism – do not eat at all after midday. Eating is regarded as necessary only to provide the body with adequate nourishment. However, you are not expected to be so austere during your home retreat session, and eating a light snack in the evening is recommended, unless you genuinely do not feel hungry.

In the two day-schedules it is suggested that your evening snack consists of a bowl of home-made vegetable soup, together with a handful of dried fruit mixed with a few freshly roasted nuts and seeds. An alternative tomato and lentil soup is more substantial than the mixed vegetable soup, and contains protein from the lentils; if you are feeling weak or hungry at this stage, this is the best option to choose.

This light meal is especially suitable during the winter, when the weather is cold and eating

A handful of finely chopped fresh herbs add flavour to a soup or sandwich filling.

something hot helps to keep the body warm. If you are undertaking your spiritual spa during the warm summer months, it is not necessary to eat hot food at this stage (although you can keep to the soup, if you like). Alternative light evening suggestions include a bowl of fresh fruit salad, a simple vegetable salad, a vegetarian sandwich made with wholemeal bread or a couple of slices of wholemeal toast – the last two offering an easy option if you are not very hungry and want a simple snack.

*Fresh, organic vegetables make a healthy and tasty soup
for a light evening meal.*

mixed vegetable soup

ingredients (all preferably organic)

1 small onion, finely chopped

a little vegetable oil

a selection of any fresh vegetables that you have in
your kitchen chopped into small cubes

method

1 Fry the onion in the vegetable oil for a few
minutes.

2 Add the fresh vegetables, with sufficient
water to cover them. Simmer for 5–10
minutes, or until the vegetables are soft. If you
are using leftover vegetables, add them to the
onion, stir for a couple of minutes and add
sufficient water to cover them. Heat through
for a few minutes.

3 Serve the soup. If you require more flavour,
stir in some finely chopped herbs, a little soy
sauce, freshly ground pepper or toasted ground
sesame seeds.

Red lentils are a good source of protein and nourishment, and make a substantial soup.

tomato and lentil soup

ingredients (all preferably organic)

1 small onion, finely sliced

a little vegetable oil

1 small carrot, grated

1 tablespoon red lentils

1 small can chopped tomatoes

method

1 Fry the onion in the vegetable oil for a few minutes.

2 Add the carrot and lentils, with sufficient water to cover them. Simmer for 15 minutes.

3 Add the tomatoes and bring the mixture to the boil.

4 Pour the soup into a blender and process for 1–2 minutes.

5 Serve the soup. If you require more flavour, stir in some finely chopped herbs, a little soy sauce, freshly ground pepper or toasted ground sesame seeds.

dried fruit, nuts and seeds

ingredients (all preferably organic)

a selection of raw, unsalted nuts, such as almonds, cashews, pistachios and walnuts

a few sunflower seeds, pine nuts and pumpkin seeds

a selection of dried fruit of your choice, such as dates, apricots, sultanas, papaya and raisins, coarsely chopped

method

1 Dry-roast the nuts and seeds for a few minutes in a small frying pan until lightly toasted, then allow them to cool for a few minutes.

2 Mix together the dried fruit in a bowl.

3 Add the nuts and seeds to the fruit, and serve.

Fresh fruit or vegetables make a healthy, vitamin-rich snack at this time of the day.

fresh fruit salad

ingredients (all preferably organic)

1 small bunch of grapes, chopped

1 medium slice of melon, chopped

1 small pear or apple, chopped

6 strawberries or raspberries

1 kiwi fruit, chopped

1 small banana, chopped

juice of ½ lemon

method

1 Mix together all the fruit in a large bowl.

2 Pour over the lemon juice and stir it in thoroughly to the fruit. Leave for 5–10 minutes to allow the different flavours to diffuse before eating the fruit salad.

Nuts and seeds contain a lot of trace minerals and provide a healthy source of protein.

vegetable salad

ingredients (all preferably organic)

½ lettuce, chopped

¼ cucumber, chopped

2 tomatoes, chopped

1 small beetroot, grated

1 small carrot, grated

1 small bunch fresh coriander or parsley, chopped

1 teaspoon mixed sunflower and sesame seeds, toasted

a little olive oil

squeeze of lemon juice

method

1 Put the lettuce, cucumber and tomatoes in a large bowl, then add the beetroot and carrot and mix well.

2 Add the herbs and toasted seeds to the bowl.

3 Add the oil and lemon juice and toss thoroughly, before serving the salad.

vegetarian sandwich or toast

ingredients

2 slices wholemeal bread (preferably organic)

butter or vegetable spread

suggested sandwich fillings: cheese or hard-boiled
egg, mixed with salad; hummus and avocado;
cottage cheese and chopped dates

suggested toast toppings: peanut butter with yeast
extract or jam; tahini with yeast extract or honey

method

1 Lightly cover your bread or toast with the butter or vegetable spread, then add your chosen filling or topping.

Wholemeal bread contains natural fibre which helps keep your digestive system healthy.

herbal teas

Suitable herbal teas for bedtime include those that are calming and relaxing, and which therefore promote a good night's sleep. Your meditation may have caused a lot of thoughts to arise, and a soothing herbal tea will calm your mind.

Several of these herbal teas have a mild diuretic action, which means that they slightly increase the production of urine. To avoid having to go to the toilet in the middle of the night, add a teaspoon of honey to your bedtime herbal tea, because honey largely counteracts the diuretic effect. If you are not familiar with herbal teas, experiment before your home retreat with the different tastes and effects; for instance, see if you like the taste of camomile tea (with or without honey) and whether it helps you to relax and sleep well.

night-time herbal teas

• Probably the best-known herbal tea for night-time is camomile, which is gently soothing and digestive.

• Vervain, lime flower, fennel, spearmint and lemon grass teas are all suitably soporific and gently aid digestion as you sleep.

• There are several proprietary night-time blends, and their ingredients may also include hawthorn berries, blackberry leaves, orange blossom and rosebuds.

• You could also try buying a range of dried herbs and creating your own special blend of bedtime herbal tea.

At the end of your home retreat day you can enjoy a cup
of calming herbal tea.

✦* relaxing exercises

Chi kung exercises can be both re-energizing and relaxing. The following exercises drawn from chi kung relax the different elements and subtle energies of the body.

This exercise gently relaxes and calms your energy as well as stretching and opening your chest, which may be cramped from sitting still in meditation. A visualized shower of sunlight washes over you, washing away any stagnant chi energy and encouraging fresh chi energy to refresh and relax your body.

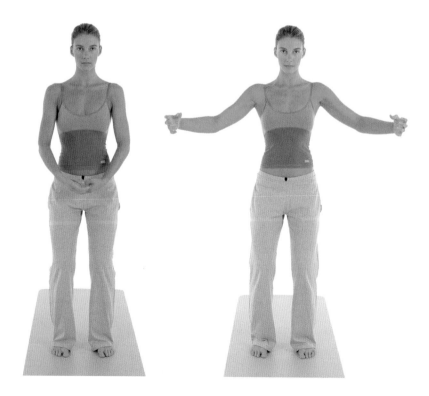

1 Start by standing on the mat with your legs hip width apart. Keep your knees relaxed and slightly bent. Let your arms hang loosely down with the hands rounded together in front of your body. Pull in your stomach and abdomen, and allow your spine to lengthen as you adjust your posture. You should end up standing relaxed with knees slightly bent, but with the upper body held erect.

2 As you slowly breathe in, begin to raise your arms upwards and out to the sides. Keep your arms soft and naturally rounded, and make sure your feet are still firmly in contact with the ground. Make sure you are looking straight ahead, as if at a distant horizon.

3 Continue raising your arms until they are above your head. Make sure you keep them relaxed and soft. Continue to inhale deeply to absorb the rising chi energy generated by the movement of your arms and the expansion of your chest, which opens out to breathe in new chi energy along with the inhaled breath.

4 When your arms have reached above your body, hold them gently still. Visualize fresh, relaxing chi energy filling your palms from the sunlight above. Stand and absorb chi for a few breaths. Then exhale and bring your arms gently down in front of your body.

5 As you move your arms downwards you bring the chi energy into your body, through your face, chest and abdomen. You can imagine the new chi energy sweeping down your body, calming and relaxing you, and clearing away any stagnant old chi energy. Keep your palms facing towards you.

6 As you slowly finish the out breath, gently lower your head and relax your jaw as your hands continue downwards to the top of your thighs. Then either repeat the exercise from the beginning or finish, feeling relaxed and ready to move on to the next home retreat activity. Repeat this exercise six to ten times.

✦✳ loving-kindness meditation

This meditation helps you connect with your natural ability to love others, and to wish them well-being and happiness.

First, you generate a feeling of loving-kindness within your heart, with awareness and sincerity. Then you direct loving-kindness systematically towards yourself, towards friends, strangers and even enemies, and eventually towards all beings everywhere. Expanding loving-kindness from yourself to others in ever-widening circles generates inner feelings of harmony and peace.

1 Set your alarm for 30 minutes. Start by sitting still in your usual meditation posture. Watch the breath in calm meditation (see page 52) for a few minutes. At the same time try to discover within your heart a warm, caring feeling towards all life.

2 Now start to develop loving-kindness towards yourself. Accept yourself as a human being: someone with both faults and good qualities, but someone who has the right to try and find happiness and avoid suffering. Perhaps sometimes you feel you don't deserve to be happy, or you judge yourself unkindly. Soften these harsh feelings and feel compassion for yourself. Remind yourself that developing loving-kindness towards yourself is the first step in developing loving-kindness towards others.

3 Silently say to yourself, 'May I live in safety. May I experience mental happiness, peace and joy, physical happiness and health. May my daily life go easily, without difficulties.' Repeat these words silently several times, and reflect on the meaning behind them. These phrases are traditionally used in loving-kindness meditation, but you can amend them, if you wish to use something more meaningful for yourself. Try to cultivate your feelings rather than your intellect; really *feel* the loving-kindness, rather than just thinking about it.

4 After a few minutes bring to mind someone who has helped you in some way. It might be a benefactor, a teacher or parent, a spouse or lover. It's important to choose someone for whom you feel great respect, love and gratitude. Repeat the above phrases, but substituting that person's name. Remember his or her great kindness towards you, and feel loving-kindness towards this person.

5 After a few minutes include a good friend – someone for whom you feel real affection – and repeat the phrases using his or her name. Now include someone towards whom you have no strong feelings, such as a stranger. This can be hard, so remind yourself that someone you do not

know has as much right as you (and everyone else) to find freedom from suffering and to achieve happiness. There is no reason not to wish this person well, so really try to generate a feeling of loving-kindness in your heart towards them.

6 Now include an enemy: someone who has harmed you, or towards whom you have very negative feelings. This is usually really difficult, so allow yourself as much time as you need. Reflect that you don't have to like this person, or condone his or her negative behaviour, but you can develop loving-kindness towards your enemy and not wish this person harm. Remember that your enemy is a complex being, with many possibly conflicting feelings and difficult circumstances that may affect the way he or she behaves. Reflect that by offering your enemy genuine loving-kindness, you might help him or her behave more considerately. Recall that sometimes you too behave badly towards others, but you would like those people to forgive you and not wish you harm.

7 Finally include all beings everywhere, and send out feelings of loving-kindness to them all. If you wish, you can visualize sending streams of loving-kindness from your heart, as white or gold light radiating out to fill the whole world. Rest in the warm feeling of all-pervasive loving-kindness for the remainder of the meditation session.

✦*watching the light fade

This simple, non-traditional meditation connects you to the ever-changing nature of reality. Sunset meditation deepens your awareness of the ephemeral beauty of the natural world and the impermanent nature of all phenomena. Depending on where you live and the time of year, you may need to swap this session with an earlier one, in order to practise this meditation as the sun sets and the light fades.

1 There is a choice of start times for this meditation: either about 20 minutes before the sun is due to set, or just as the sun is setting. Either time is effective: the sinking sun is the object of concentration in the first option, and the fading light and colour changes in the second. Select the option you prefer, work out your start time and adjust your schedule accordingly.

2 After setting your alarm for the usual 30 minutes, sit comfortably in front of a west-facing window or open door. Watch your breath in calm meditation (see page 52) for a few minutes, but also keep your eyes open and focused on the setting sun or fading light. These are very different objects of concentration from watching the breath, and you may notice that your mind partly wanders off into thoughts and fantasies. Try to focus all your attention (and not simply your eyes) on the setting sun or fading light.

3 Observe how the colours around the setting sun subtly change from moment to moment, or how the fading light constantly shifts in shade and tone. Watch as the power and beauty of Nature change before your eyes, and as day becomes night while the world turns.

4 Reflect on how the modern world with electric light has changed the natural rhythm of life. Our ancestors rose with the sunrise and went to bed at sunset in perfect harmony with the seasons and Nature. As you watch the sun sink or the light fade, try to reconnect with these natural rhythms of existence.

5 Watch for the moment when the sun actually sinks below the horizon, or when dusk falls, reminding you that you are nearly at the end of your home-retreat day and will soon be undertaking the day's remaining activities

A beautiful sunset is a wonderful object of meditation,
and keeps you in touch with Nature.

and meditations. You may feel a sense of tranquillity as you hear the wind in the trees or the tiny sounds of birds, insects and other animals preparing for the night.

6 When your alarm rings, spend a few moments simply enjoying your inner peace and calm before moving on to the next item on your home-retreat schedule.

✦✱ mantra meditation

Mantra meditation and chanting (see page 122) are quite similar practices. The main difference is that you chant out loud, whereas mantras are usually recited under the breath, using prayer beads to count each mantra recitation.

You may have experience of chanting or of mantra recitation, or even be familiar with both. In that case you will know which of the two practices you would prefer to do during your home retreat. If you are not familiar with either, simply choose one, or experiment with both and then decide which method you prefer.

1 First, choose between the Christian mantra 'maranatha' and the Buddhist mantra 'om mani padme hum'.

2 *Maranatha* is an Aramaic word meaning 'Come Lord, come Lord Jesus.' This mantra practice originated with the early Desert Fathers, and was developed and extensively practised by the Romanian-born monk John Cassian during the 5th century.

Alternatively, you may choose the Buddhist mantra, 'om mani padme hum'. This is difficult to paraphrase exactly, but the words are often translated as 'jewel in the lotus'. This cryptic, mystical phrase refers to the awakened qualities of Buddha Shakyamuni, and pays homage to him for awakening to the true nature of existence.

3 To practise the mantra 'maranatha', start by sitting and watching the breath in calm meditation for a few minutes. Then gradually start to slowly but continuously repeat the word 'maranatha' under your breath, using prayer beads. Make sure you give equal stress to each of the four syllables, – 'mar-a-nath-a'. As you repeat the word continuously, try to focus your whole attention on the mantra.

To practise the Buddhist mantra 'om mani padme hum', follow the instructions above, slowly and continuously repeating the mantra under your breath. If you find yourself distracted by thoughts, stop, spend a few minutes in calm meditation and then resume repeating the mantra.

4 When the alarm rings, stop the mantra recitation. Spend a few minutes in silent contemplation before moving on.

Mantra meditation is a devotional practice in both Christianity and Buddhism.

✦* sleep-promoting bath

Although bathing is normally a routine activity, during your spiritual spa you can turn the simple act of taking a bath into a meaningful ritual. This is like meditation in many ways, with the same purpose of keeping the mind focused.

In meditation, the object of concentration is usually the breath, whereas here it is a series of activities performed with a sense of purpose. While you are preparing and taking your bath with essential oils, you need to remain focused and aware of your actions and feelings.

There is quite a range of calming essential oils that are suitable for an evening bath. As you prepare for your bath, meditate for a few minutes to assess how you are feeling, to ensure you select the most therapeutic essential oils for your current state of mind. All the oils suggested here promote restful sleep, but each one has its own unique character and therapeutic effect on the mind, body and emotions. Lavender is a traditional oil for evening relaxation but you may prefer to use one or more of the oils suggested. Using an essential oil and a herbal tea derived from the same herb reinforces its therapeutic action; for example, you can use camomile essential oil in the bath and drink camomile tea afterwards.

Allow your senses to help you select the essential oils. Sniff each oil that comes to mind during your meditation, and you will soon know if it's one of the right oils for you to use. Choose two or three essential oils, and use a maximum of six to eight drops in total. For example, two drops of lavender, three drops of camomile and three drops of neroli makes a light floral blend; two drops of clary sage, two drops of melissa and three drops of sandalwood gives a deeper, warmer aroma.

calming essential oils

- Lavender is a traditional favourite for an evening bath, because it is gentle and relaxing and promotes sleep.

- Neroli is delicate, quietening and refreshing.

- Camomile is soothing, tranquil and restful.

- Marjoram and clary sage are warming and calming.

- Sandalwood, melissa, mandarin and frankincense help to slow racing thoughts.

Make sure you drop the essential oils into your bath just before getting in.

*To make your bathing ritual a special experience, light
some candles and turn off the electric lights.*

1 Start to run the water for your bath. Light
candles and place them around the
bathroom, then turn off the electric light.

2 Choose a beautiful object that holds spiritual
significance for you, and place it where you
can see it from the bath. It might be a statue of
Buddha or some other religious icon, a crystal or
a vase of flowers.

3 You might like to play some music quietly,
such as Gregorian chant, spiritual, New Age
or classical music. Silence is also good.

4 Once the bath is full, carefully drop in your
chosen essential oils and agitate the water to
disperse them thoroughly.

*Take time to relax deeply in your bath and enjoy the
fragrance of the essential oils.*

5 Climb into the bath slowly. Be aware of each
sensation as it occurs: feel the water swirling
around your body, notice the water temperature
and how the experience of immersing yourself
makes you feel. Observe how the essential oils
have an immediate impact on your senses, and
then how the effect gradually fades.

6 Take a bowl or pitcher, or cup your hands, and slowly pour a stream of water over your head. Do this mindfully for a few minutes, noticing the sensations as the water touches your skin. This form of ritual ablution is traditionally used to cleanse the aura and the psyche, and feels refreshing. It helps to disperse any troubled thoughts that may have surfaced in your meditation sessions during the day.

7 Lie back and enjoy the sensation of the warm water and the therapeutic effect of the oils. Breathe deeply, and watch your thoughts arise and drift away for as long as you wish.

8 When you have finished your bath, dry yourself carefully and put on a warm bathrobe to keep you warm for your final meditation sessions.

✦✱ chanting

If you prefer to chant out loud, rather than recite mantras quietly under your breath, you will probably prefer this ritual to the quieter mantra meditation described on page 116.

This popular form of chanting belongs to the Nichiren Shoshu school of Buddhism, founded by the 13th-century priest Nichiren Daishonin. The lay organization of Nichiren Shoshu is known as the Sokka Gakai and has many international members, although the majority come from Japan, where the school originated.

Members are formally given their own copy of the Dai Gohonzon – the phrase, or mantra, 'Namu-myoho-renge-kyo' – as part of their joining ritual. Local groups meet regularly for group chanting sessions, although members are expected to chant the mantra twice daily. However, during your home retreat even one session will give you a taste of the spiritual potency of chanting.

1 Set your alarm for 30 minutes, then sit and watch the breath in calm meditation (see page 52) for a few minutes.

2 Now start to chant the mantra 'Namu-myoho-renge-kyo' out loud. The pronunciation is much as written, except that the 'h' in 'myoho' is silent and 'renge' is pronounced 'rengi'. Choose a pace and rhythm that suit you, because one of the purposes of chanting is to connect with your natural inner rhythm.

3 Continue chanting the mantra for the duration of the session. You may notice a slight hypnotic effect, but try to keep a clear, focused awareness on your chanting practice. If you become distracted, spend a few minutes in calm meditation, then return to chanting.

4 When the alarm rings, spend a few minutes calmly watching the breath before moving on to the next home-retreat session.

Chanting allows you the opportunity to express yourself through your voice.

✦✱ closing prayers

If neither the chanting practice nor the mantra recitation appeals to you, an alternative is simply to choose a prayer that is meaningful to you from one of the many prayers of different religions.

1 Set your alarm for 30 minutes, then start the prayer session with a few minutes of calm meditation (see page 52).

2 Recite your chosen prayer, either out loud or under your breath, as you prefer.

3 Alternate between a few minutes of meditation and a few minutes of prayer until the session ends.

You might like to try the short prayer set out below, which is a favourite of many Tibetan Buddhists and gives them great inspiration. It embodies the spirit of compassion for all living beings.

Tibetan prayer

For as long as space endures,
And for as long as living beings remain,
Until then may I, too, abide
To dispel the misery of the world.

Saying prayers at the end of the day is a lovely end to your home retreat.

a review of the day

At the end of the day it's a good idea to undertake a review. This means making an honest, clear appraisal of how the entire day went for you. Do not be judgemental: you should neither beat yourself up for not completing every meditation or exercise perfectly, nor praise yourself for being so dutiful that you experienced a perfect home retreat. Judgements like this have no value.

A clear appraisal of how things went for you – without judging your experience in any way – is a useful exercise. Your review should include a brief scan through every meditation session, exercise, rest period, and so on. Simply note mentally your experience of each session. If some experiences were positive, then you can rest assured that you were well prepared for these sessions and were diligent in completing them. However, rather than being too self-congratulatory, simply accept them with gratitude, and without creating any expectation that next time you do them you will have an equally good experience.

If some of your meditations or exercises were not so positive, try to understand why this might be. Analyse these experiences, without feeling negative about having had some less successful sessions. Perhaps you had not prepared yourself adequately, or you daydreamed and did not follow the meditation technique for very long during the session. Whatever you discover about these experiences can be useful the next time you undertake a meditation retreat. Simply accept that some of your sessions did not go particularly well. Even the most experienced meditator can have negative experiences; the trick, after a review, is to simply let them go.

planning and preparing for tomorrow

After the review of your day as you lie in bed, it's time to turn your mind to tomorrow, just before you go to sleep. Either you will be returning to your normal everyday life, or you will be undertaking another home-retreat day. In either case it is a good idea to prepare yourself mentally for what tomorrow is likely to bring.

If today has been a one-day retreat, or is the end of a home retreat, then tomorrow you will be returning to all the tasks, activities and relationships that normal life entails. One of the main things you will notice is that the all-encompassing silence you have experienced during your spiritual spa will come to an end. Your daily life may at first appear rather raucous, although after a few hours the noise levels will seem quite normal to you. You may also notice a slight reluctance in yourself to engage in conversation, perhaps followed by the desire to talk at great length.

These are quite normal post-retreat experiences and are nothing to worry about; simply be aware that such reactions may occur. Try to avoid telling other people about your retreat, unless they are also meditators who have some understanding of what you are talking about. After a short time your usual lifestyle will seem absolutely normal, and your home retreat will fade into the past.

If you will be spending another day in meditation, as part of a longer home retreat, reflect that tomorrow will be similar to the day that has just ended and that you will be spending most of your time in sitting and movement meditations. Just as you did before your first home-retreat day, check your motivation and remind yourself of this precious opportunity to spend time meditating and reconnecting with your spiritual essence. Try not to have too many expectations of what tomorrow's sessions may bring; each time you meditate your experience will be subtly different.

Take some time last thing at night to reflect on your experiences and plan for the following day.

index

acknowledgements

Special Photography: © Octopus Publishing Group Limited
/Russell Sadur.

Other Photography: Imagesource 16.

Octopus Publishing Group Limited/Frank Adam 86; /Steven
Conroy 108; /Gus Filgate 89; /Mike Hemsley 93; /Jeremy
Hopley 106 bottom right; /David Jordan 57; /Sandra Lane 84
bottom right, 104; /William Lingwood 105; /Neil Mersh 56;
/Peter Myers 39; /Ian Parsons 37; /Lis Parsons 84 bottom left,
88 bottom left; /Peter Pugh-Cook 14, 17, 27, 48 left, 48 right,
48 centre, 48 top right, 49 top centre, 49 top left, 49 bottom
right, 49 bottom left, 49 bottom centre, 50 top centre, 50 top
left, 50 top right, 50 centre right, 50 centre left, 50 bottom
right, 51 top centre, 51 top left, 51 top right, 51 bottom right,
51 bottom left, 51 bottom centre, 66 bottom right, 66 bottom
left, 67 top centre, 67 top left, 67 top right, 98 left, 98 right,
99 top left, 99 top right, 99 bottom, 110 bottom right, 110
bottom left, 111, 111 top centre, 111 top right, 111 bottom
right; /William Reavell 72; /Simon Smith 77; /Ian Wallace 64;
/Mark Winwood 20, 22.

Photodisc 7, 15, 71, 107, 115.

Executive Editor Brenda Rosen
Editor Emma Pattison
Executive Art Editor Sally Bond
Designer Elizabeth Healey
Picture Library Manager Jennifer Veall
Production Manager Louise Hall